Listen

By the same author

Folly River
Richard Wilbur's Creation (editor)

Listen

A MEMOIR

Wendy Salinger

BLOOMSBURY

Author's Note: Because remembering is an act of the imagination, the only real name I've used in this book is my own.

Two passages from this book were published in slightly different form by *The Kenyon Review*, Volume XIX, Number 1, winter 1997.

Quotations in "Undoing the Spell" are taken from *Circus Time* by Marion Conser, New York, 1948, Simon and Schuster.

Published by Bloomsbury Publishing, New York and London
Distributed to the trade by Holtzbrinck Publishers

All papers used by Bloomsbury Publishing are natural, recyclable products made from wood grown in well-managed forests. The manufacturing processes conform to the environmental regulations of the country of origin.

Library of Congress Cataloging-in-Publication Data

Salinger, Wendy.
Listen : a memoir / Wendy Salinger.—1st U.S. ed.
p. cm.
ISBN-13: 978–1–59691–083–6 (hardcover)
ISBN-10: 1–59691–083–6 (hardcover)

1. Salinger, Wendy—Childhood and youth. 2. Poets, American—20th century—Biography. 3. Poets, American—20th century—Family relationships. 4. College teachers—United States—Family relationships. 5. Fathers and daughters—United States. I. Title.
PS3569.A45953Z468 2006
811'.54—dc22
2005017493

First U.S. Edition 2005

1 3 5 7 9 10 8 6 4 2

Typeset by Hewer Text UK Ltd, Edinburgh
Printed in the United States of America by Quebecor World Fairfield

For my sisters and my mother,
and for Jane

Memory for never-discussed events is likely to be qualitatively different from memory for events that have been discussed.

—Jennifer Freyd, *Betrayal Trauma*

A man may see how this world goes with no eyes.
Look with thine ears.

—*King Lear*

Prologue

I'm sure he's miserable, she says when I call, tonight he took my hand and put it on his cheek, that's the first time he's done anything like that, he never liked the way I touch him, now he's in such pitiful shape all he wants is to be petted, he keeps saying, "You don't know what terrible pain I'm in."

I can't tell you whether to come yet or not, you have to make your own decision, set your own priorities in life, I don't know if he'll be here in the morning.

They watch him every second now, he tries to climb out of bed, I was there, I went to help get him back in but he pushed me away, it's amazing how much strength there still is in those arms, I had to laugh when he shoved me like that, Dr. Barbour was there so I laughed, I said, "That's the old Victor, that's the Victor I know," they see what I go through, I don't say anything but they see.

I had to help him to the sink to urinate, I put my arm around his chest, he's so thin, I could feel the heart beating and his eyes so wild and pathetic.

He still recognizes me, they keep asking if he still recognizes me.

All the doctors have been wonderful, I told that young one what's-his-name who comes in, I said, "You have a healing touch, you have healing in your hands," I could tell he liked that.

Father Tom came by on Sunday to administer the Sacrament, our family's always been special to him, he knew how much it would mean but your father just stared at him without a word, Tom finally had to ask, "Do you know who I am, do you recognize me?" and Daddy said, "I know who you are, I'm just trying to figure out how to get you to get me out of here."

He says he's never been so mistreated in his life, he told me the nurses sneer at him and pull his leg, they raise their voices, he said I was his only friend, he ordered me, "You've got to get me out of here, if I stay here it will be my death warrant," I cried, it's the first time I've ever had to disobey him, I said, "I can't do that, I'm afraid I won't be able to take care of you by myself."

His voice is still strong when he's angry, the nurses say he still might fool us.

They've promised they won't release him to go home this way though, the doctors don't even talk about it anymore, it's just in his mind, it's the mental confusion that's what's so sad, it's true what they say, you know, about Shakespeare's ages of man, it really is a return to childhood, he eats with his fingers now and the words come out all wrong, they say they'll try to keep him with us as long as they can.

Yesterday he started singing, all of a sudden with the nurse right there, the whole of the twenty-third psalm, I cried, I told him I didn't know it had been set to music.

Just days ago he was trying to recite *Faust, Part 1*, to test his memory, that's all beyond him now.

It's hard for me, it would be easier with one of you here to spell me, he's always had attendants, the man's never been alone in his life.

One of his girls came by the other day to see him, you know her, what's-her-name who works in the campus bookstore, the nurses told me they thought she was a daughter, you can imagine how it made me look.

Well, you have to remember the good things, I kept thinking he might say something at the end, like the song, you know the one, that movie was so popular, how love means you'll finally apologize, my own father was so good, so thoughtful when he died, he just said, "I hope you have a good life," well, it's too late now, you can't look back but it's something to think about, maybe it could help you in your own life.

2

I don't know what to tell him, if you could see the pleading look in his eyes, so appealing, he asked me, "Why am I being punished?" I tried to reason with him, I said, "Your brother never thought that, Frank never said he was being punished at the end," but he stuck out his tongue at me, a nurse witnessed the whole thing.

There was some Charlie Chaplin program on night before last, I thought I caught him watching for a minute, he was making faces at the TV, maybe it was meant for me.

Both of Frank's daughters were with him at the end, of course, and they had children to leave, but you have your own lives, your own commitments, your sisters have husbands to think about, you have a job, Frank's girls didn't work, they've never had a full-time job in their lives, I just don't want the three of you to have to go through this kind of thing with me, I don't want heroic measures, I've always been so healthy, I keep waiting for the ax to fall.

Well, it's not the horror of cancer, I've watched so many of my friends go through the horror of cancer with their husbands.

I do think we should plan what to wear just in case, form's always mattered to your father, maybe a dark skirt with a simple linen blouse if I can find a linen blouse, you three can just wear nice dresses, Clare has a lovely blue one she wore the last time she was here, I might get a hat too, a little black one with a veil like they used to wear, I think I could pull it off, if one of you came down you could take me to that new mall out toward Raleigh, they have such nice stores, I haven't had a chance to do any shopping, my secretaries have been so busy, and I need new slipcovers for the chairs in the living room, there'll be people coming over, Daddy would want things to look nice, I've always kept a nice home for him.

Well, we'll see when you get here, we really have to stop now, even with the low rates at this hour it mounts up when you go on and on, you'll need the money for plane fare, I don't know what it is, you can figure it out, call some of the airlines and compare, you'll have to decide, people feel guilty at a time like this when money's a consideration, I just don't know if you want to see him one last time.

Part 1

Life Before Death

Early on one frosty morn
(every morning)
his frosted eyebrows
his bluebird pajamas
his mind on something else
Begin again Finnegan
Whiskers on his chin again.

The Table Setter

"She's not eating.

"Lillian?

"Would you pay some attention to your daughter? She hasn't touched a thing on her plate."

"She's eating, Victor. Look. She finished almost all of the potato."

"She's picking at it. That's not eating. Do we have to go through the same thing every night? Is she sick, or is she just being lazy? Everyone else is finished. Stick your fork *into* the food. You want me to show you how it's done? Do you need to be fed like a baby?"

"Wendy, your father's telling you to eat."

"Maybe there's something wrong with it. Is there something you don't like about the food? If you don't like what's put in front of you, speak to your mother. She's in charge of food preparation, I'm just the provider. That's what I do in this family, I write the checks."

"You heard your father, do you want all his hard-earned checks to go to waste?"

"Can it, Lillian. Just shut your trap. You think I don't recognize a dig like that? The way you try to undermine me. A child could spot your tricks."

"I only want to make sure she appreciates the sacrifices you make for this family."

"I'm not asking her to absorb a goddamn philosophy lesson, Lillian. I just want her to eat her dinner."

"It's true though. People don't realize. They think professors teach their two or three classes a day and then have all that free time. They don't understand about the other demands and pressures you have in your position."

"Oh there's a can of worms, lady! You just said a mouthful, and you know it. You want to talk about who spends time doing what for this family? The shopping and the errands, all the chauffeuring, this girl to that lesson, that one to this. Compared to mine, your day's a bloody picnic. Sitting behind that typewriter with a cup of coffee gossiping with a bunch of other hens sitting behind *their* type-writers."

"I've never complained about my secretarial jobs, Victor, you know that. I've always gone to an office. I know we need the extra income."

"You want to quit? Quit. Play golf. If you can figure out how. Join the Valley matrons at the country club and sit on your ass all day. You think I care which gaggle of females you choose to waste your time with?"

"You know I'd never do such a thing, we can't afford to join the country club, I've told the girls that."

"Oh and that's my fault of course, that's what you're telling them. We can't afford to join the country club because their father doesn't make as much money as his swell neighbors."

"I'd never say that, they wouldn't dare think it. They know how underpaid professors are. People don't value what they do, they don't appreciate the value of a liberal education in this country anymore."

"I'll tell you who's doing the underappreciating, you that's who. You think typing eighty words a minute is comparable to teaching *The Sorrows of Young Werther*. You think it puts you on a par with me. You're the one whose values are skewed, Lillian. Screwed. You couldn't keep a family in garbage bags on the pittance you make. You couldn't keep your daughters in sanitary napkins once all four of your vaginas are operating at capacity in a few years."

"I know it's only a secondary income, Victor. To help us get by.

I've always understood the needs of the academic way of life, you taught me. We've never been able to have me stay home with the girls."

"Needs? You talk about needs? Whose needs do you think we're discussing? Do I ever express any needs? I haven't had a new suit or a decent overcoat in five years. It's always, 'Victor, I *need* a new sofa.' 'I *need* a chair for the living room to go with the little footstool in the boudoir.' Honestly Lillian, you're going to destroy half the forests in the South with your obsession for furniture. As it is you inherited half my grandmother's priceless Victorian pieces when you married me, but apparently that doesn't satisfy you. It doesn't interest you. You've never cared about the past. There's always some 'darling' new furniture outlet with some kind of 'darling' neocolonial deacon's bench in the window. Christ. You're going to turn this place into a miniature Williamsburg. You call it neocolonial, I call it *faux*. *Pseudo-pseudo, faux-faux*, that's what I say. *Ersatz*, lady—from the German, if you remember."

"It's for your sake, Victor, I only do it for you and the girls. I want them to have a nice home so they can bring their friends over. I know how important it is for a department chairman to keep up appearances."

"Bullshit. That's what I said, *bullshit*. And don't give me that look. I can say what I like in my own house."

"I only meant I've never forgotten what you taught me all those years ago in Iowa. I was too young and inexperienced back then to understand. I didn't know about the front professors have to put up for one another, all the maneuvering and the dinner parties, you had to teach me just the way you'd taught Mia but I never forgot."

"You think you can get away with that? Take yourself out of it and leave me holding the bag? Bag of garbage is what it is. Mouthful of misrepresentation. You don't deck this place out like a furniture showroom for my sake or the girls', you never have. You do it to keep up with the Joneses. And the Smiths. And the Perrys and the Picketts, and every other two-car, split-level family in the Valley. Not to mention the faculty wives over in the Forest with their suffocating *mitteleuropa* taste. What will the neighbors think, the other wives, the other mothers of the other two-point-two children that's what's always mattered to you. How things look. Not what your husband's needs are or your family's. Always the outside, never the inside. 'The outward and visible sign' not 'the inward and spiritual grace,' those are your values, Lillian, they always have been. So don't play the innocent with me. You weren't a *tabula rasa* when I married you. You got what you wanted. What galls me is that it wasn't enough. It never is. There's always something more. Something I'm not providing you with. New sofa, new chairs, new clothes. Out with the old, in with the new, that's what you live by. You'll be that way the day they cart me off to the junkyard with the rest of your castoffs. And the day after."

"I try to look nice for you. I try to put in a good appearance. I know how much it means to you to be with a good-looking woman."

"Shut up, Lillian! You'd better watch your mouth! You think you can sneak around me like that and turn this into something else? You're heading for deep waters, watch out you don't get in over your head."

"I was only following the conversation, Victor. About your needs."

"I said shut up, didn't I? This 'conversation' is over, and you know damn well it wasn't about any needs of *mine*. It's your needs that call the tune in this family, Lillian. Your need to find one more opportunity to humiliate me at the head of my own dinner table. Another demonstration of my deficiencies for the benefit of one of our daughters, that's your idea of the wifely thing to do, isn't it? Let a man know he's not a man. I'm so inadequate my wife has to join the workforce and sit behind a typewriter like a drone every day from nine till five. I'm a failure as a breadwinner and a man. Is that about it? Does that pretty well sum it up for you?"

"I know what a hard life you have, poor man. I never forget for a minute."

"Don't even try it, lady. This show's over. I've had a bellyful. If you want to add to my misery, you'll have to knock on the door of my study. I've got a stack of blue books this high waiting for me, I never have a minute for my own poetry, and there are translation proofs that have been on my desk for a week. Not that that entitles me to any extra consideration around here. After all I only bring in a lousy professor's salary."

"What about the rest of the dinner I prepared? Should I make her finish what's left on her plate?"

"Do whatever the hell you want, I don't care. Let her go to her room and finish her homework with the others. Let her starve. You can all starve as far as I'm concerned. I wash my hands. The hunter-gatherer comes home to his lair with an expensive filet mignon, and they're still not satisfied. God knows I don't begin to understand the female appetite."

Cleanup

She stacks the plates. Casts utensils on top, the dirty in with the clean. It makes a punishing sound on the dead air, the lull where he quit the room. She doesn't speak, won't look up, her eyes hooded, chin pressed down, making more chins from the flesh softening at her neck.

Perfect skin. Poured but contained like the cold cream in the jar on her dressing table.

Back and forth to the kitchen she makes grim trips, her tread heavy. Her limbs lift through a watery medium as if, burdened with more than the load of tableware, she means to signify to a larger, more discerning audience than the one embodied in me, an eleven-year-old sitting motionless in front of the plate of her half-eaten dinner.

A mash of cold peas, cold potato, the meat with its missing wedge.

She works around me, clearing other people's settings, removing the serving dishes, the platter, salt and pepper shakers, breadbasket.

She circles a final time, scouting the clear spaces. Just the one place left. She reaches around from behind my back to take the plate.

"Never marry a man like your father," she warns me.

Car Ride

He drove us. No one else could. He's little behind the rim of the wheel, only five-foot-six. It's the head that dominates, the fixity of his gaze. The muscle popping in his jaw, the monoxide of the lecture. His neck hunkers down inside his raincoat, the gray needles of his hair where it's grown too long pricking the collar. He's had to cancel the barber again, had to sacrifice his own needs to ours—again.

"I told you to make a list. Why do you never remember? If you expect me to organize your day properly, you have to make a list."

In the passenger seat, Mother keeps her eyes forward.

The windshield wipers land heavy blows, like the sound of cutlery falling on the silence at the dinner table. They make a part in the wall of water so the plastic bubble of the family can move through. Gray soak, pigeon splat, wet brown leaves. We're sealed against all weather. The world slides off the windshield and fractures in his glasses. No sound can reach the outside.

"What did you say? Did you say something, Lillian? You're mumbling. You do that deliberately to annoy me, don't you. Speak up if you're going to interrupt. You know I can't concentrate on the driving and listen to your jabbering at the same time. It's giving me a splitting headache."

He has a headache. He has a stiff neck from driving—no one will rub it for him, *she* never even offers.

"Watch out!" She grabs the armrest beside her. Her right foot grinds into the rubber floor mat, her body pulling back against the strain of operating the imaginary brake.

He stomps on the real brake, the wheel jerks under his hands, and the whole company of passengers swerves to the left. A dark shape like our own, a hull, looms out of the weather across the occluded screen of our vision.

"Why did you do that! Why did you yell at me? I've told you never to yell at the person behind the wheel! Do you want to get yourself killed?"

"I thought you didn't see him."

"I saw him, what's the matter with you? I've been driving for over forty years, have I ever endangered your life—any of you? Well, have I?"

"No, of course not."

"Then why are you gripping the door handle like a maniac?"

"I'm not gripping it, I'm just resting my hand there."

"You don't have any faith in me, do you, any of you. As a driver or anything else."

"Of course we do. None of us would ever think of criticizing your driving. That man should have slowed down when he saw you pulling out."

"What do you know about it? Are you the expert here?"

We lived inside the car. It was like another room of the house, the one that moved with us wherever we moved, that took us through life.

There were two great passages, the trip to Europe, when Clare and I were in high school and Margaret stayed home to start college, and the one almost a decade earlier, in 1955, when Daddy moved the family to North Carolina. He took a summer off for that, driving east and south across the map from Iowa with many stopovers, as if to emphasize the divide in our lives, making a sightseeing tour of it as well.

It was educational, all trips were. Mother alert at her post calling off the roadside markers—battlefield sites, birthplaces of former presidents, quaint Episcopal churches where it could take up to half an hour to decipher the inscriptions on the old stones in the graveyards. When we stopped in St. Louis to see Mama, Daddy's mother, at the nursing home, it was too hot for words. She could only signal by blinking her eyes at us—once, twice, twice—where we stood looking in through the bars of her crib. Then it was on through the bluegrass of Kentucky to "My Old Kentucky Home," where Daddy paid for a photograph of the three of us with an old man strumming a banjo, a Negro. Mother wanted it for our first family Christmas card from the South.

Each girl had her place in the back seat—me on the right behind my mother, Clare at the left window with the view of the back of Daddy's head, Margaret between us. We made a game of debating which way Daddy's hair was going, black or gray? Salt or pepper? But mostly we kept quiet. The car was another place to behave, not to move while being moved. We counted cows and license plates like any normal family. Sometimes Mother asked me to sing—I had a high sweet voice, like a boy soprano. "Tammy," "If I Loved You," "When You Walk Through a Storm" were some of her favorites. She swung her head with the tune and hummed along, chin lifted, eyes closed so it was as dark for her as it was in the song and she too could have been mounting some hill and walking bravely toward whatever might come.

When we switched places for naps, Margaret moved to the front seat and Clare and I curled up in back, one of us in Mother's lap. When I stuck my thumb in my mouth, Mother shook her head and pulled it back out, then, at my pleading look, checked my father's sight line in the rearview mirror and relented.

From the Skyline Drive at Gatlinburg, Tennessee, we took the Parkway down the vaporing Smoky Mountains, Mother sucking in her breath at the hairpin curves while Daddy recited Stonewall Jackson's last words—"Let us cross over the river and rest under the shade of the trees"—as he drove us deeper and deeper into the orange clay of North Carolina, the matted kudzu and tangled roots.

In the South there was a history lesson with every mile. The past was right under our feet, scarcely buried; he always had something to show us. From our new hometown to the site of General Johnston's surrender to Sherman was only a twenty-minute drive. And we could make weekend pilgrimages over the Virginia border to the places sacred to the life of Daddy's boyhood hero, Robert E. Lee. On the rolling campus lawn of Washington and Lee Mother set up a picnic between the bronze forelegs of Lee's horse Traveller. He gave us shade and kept his faithful watch over our heads, surveying the endlessly defeating distances of the Blue Ridge Mountains from blank horse sockets.

Daddy found Lee's boyhood home in Alexandria impeccably maintained, though the elderly woman who led us through the rooms said there were so few visitors these days it was shameful. Lee's countenance seemed to hover in all the windows, Daddy wrote in a poem. At Arlington too he felt the presence of the general looking out from behind the pillars, casting long shadows over the domino rows of headstones. Kind eyes in an iron visage. Blue like Daddy's own. He said there was forgiveness in Lee's gaze, pardon for the country that never pardoned him, sorrow for the Union dead who disrupted his front yard. "Backward looking, dear Defender," Daddy called him when he wrote about Matthew Brady's photograph of the old man with spectacles perched on top of his head.

It was harder to find any history when we lived in Iowa, nothing went back much further than the previous century. Our parents had done the best they could—taking us on tours of church graveyards, an abandoned one-room schoolhouse, an agricultural museum. Every other week Daddy drove thirty miles to the liquor store in Montezuma because Marshall County was dry. Sometimes he chose one girl to accompany him—Margaret for her good behavior, Clare because she was the youngest, always complaining she hadn't been given a turn. Once, in the first grade, when I pretended to be sick at school, he came straight from his morning class to pick me up. I flung myself at him, shouting, "Ride to Montezuma!"—forgetting my carefully constructed ruse for escaping the arithmetic lesson. His tweed jacket held the comforting smells of libraries and pipe tobacco. He was always available for rescues. Mother had to be at her desk at work, typing.

Alone in the car with one of us, he had countless stories of life in the olden days in St. Louis and the malapropisms of Barbara the German cook, who spoke to spirits of the family's dead relatives while she served the living at their dinner table. It was a privilege to sit up front with him, even if some of his talk went over a child's head and on and on. His glasses held up a second windshield for the streaming scenery. The whole width of the world poured through, divided in half and flowed on, passing us by.

Every year on Christmas Eve he drove the family to Des Moines for midnight mass at St. Andrew's, an hour each way. Services there were High Church, unlike the parish in Marshall, all the things my mother loved—the sung liturgy, the long form on all the prayers, the dusty fragrance of the incense filling the nave when Father B swung the censer. She'd grown up Evangelical and Reform in Albany but decided to strike out on her own when she was a teenager, interviewing priests and pastors from all denominations before she chose one. She almost went Catholic. Daddy's family wasn't anything. He joined the Episcopal Church after they moved to Iowa, making his Confirmation in a service at St. Andrew's—a long and scrupulous spiritual journey, he explained, from that awesome moment when he'd heard the news of the Hiroshima bombing and raced to the cathedral in Mainz, where he sank to his knees to pray for all mankind.

In June we packed our summer wardrobes for the trip to Madison, where Daddy taught both sessions of summer school to supplement the meager salary Marshall College gave its assistant professors. We rented homes from the underpaid Madison professors who were teaching summer school at other institutions. Up and back we took in edifying sights—the Wisconsin Dells, Indian mounds, a dairy farm with barns and outbuildings of milk-white clapboard where we heard a lecture on pasteurization and homogenization. We stopped for a Children's Day at Little Switzerland, a whole town built on a juvenile scale. There was a carnival with low-flying, two-seater planes and a train of open cars that chugged along at a safe few miles per hour.

The rides at Candyland in Chicago were better. One summer and then a second after that, Daddy drove us there to visit his brother and his family, our cousins Hadley—a year older than Margaret—and

Kate—a year older than me. Usually both he and Mother frowned at how Uncle Frank let his girls run wild. But Uncle Frank's company put Daddy in a good mood, and at the carnival he set us free to join them in their loosely supervised adventures. Tilting machines, the giant ferris wheel—Mother had to shut her eyes and turn her back.

The trip to Spillville was more to our parents' taste. We made a detour on the way to Madison the year that marked the sixtieth anniversary of Dvořák's sojourn in that Iowa town, where he did not compose the symphony *From the New World* in D (it was already written when he arrived though some of the parts still needed to be copied) but did begin and finish the *American* quartet, Opus. 96 as well as the piano quintet Opus. 97. We saw his studio, on the second floor of a museum filled with clocks, then paid a visit to the marvel of Spillville, the World's Smallest Church.

They could make an excursion out of almost nothing. When the early Iowa summer baked the boards of our house like a pressure cooker and Daddy was about to reach his own boiling point, Mother would coax him into a drive out beyond the town limits to visit the pigs. Almost immediately we were past the backward WELCOME TO MARSHALL sign and heading into flattened distance, on a parallel with the monotone of the cornfields, cracked and dried under the first blow of the season, barely sprouted, like rows of baby teeth. Nothing to see— "no real scenery in Iowa," they always said. Dust on every surface inside the car and coming at us through the rolled-down windows. He drove in dead silence, the weight of his temper another layer on the thickness of the afternoon. Mother humored him with false gaiety, trying to trick him out of his black mood that way he hated for her to do.

Miles of nothing and then a rich stench invaded the car. That was the cue for one of us to pipe up from the back seat, "Pigs! Pigs!"

He slowed reluctantly, pulled over to the shoulder.

We lowered ourselves from the high step of the pot-boiling car, not touching the sizzling round fenders, then stood together at the wire enclosure, hands careful between the barbs, watching the hairy snouts shove and crowd each other at their trough, considering the ugly, snuffling sounds the pigs made that were like a sucking swamp.

17

Taking a Walk

No, there were four miscarriages not three, she corrects me, one for every house we lived in, remember the last time? Victor was at her bedside every minute when he didn't have class, he told her afterward her last words were "Take care of the girls," well, would have been her last words if she hadn't pulled through, she never had a single problem till the first miscarriage, three perfect babies, neighbors would stop her on the street, such attractive little girls, dressed like stair steps.

She still thinks about those long evenings back in Iowa, how she used to take us for our walk up to the playground at Oak Street Park and back, Victor sent her out after supper, he said it would clear her head, that must have been when the medication was kicking in she realizes now, the tranquilizer or whatever it was, it would have started around that time of day, the feeling of things moving in on her, afraid she was going to die, she just took what she was told to.

It's sad really, remembering, the naïve young mother with her three little girls, Clare skipping and running out in front with Margaret, me lagging behind, wobbling on those spindly legs, she had to call to Margaret to get them to slow down and wait for us.

Well, there are problems with every child, each one comes with her own set of requirements, you never know till they get here, then you forget all about it, you forget the pain, that's how nature intended, you're ready to do it all again.

It's hard on young mothers though, she can't help feeling sorry for them when she sees one on the street.

You learn with the first child, that was Margaret's burden poor thing, she was such a serious little girl, worried really, a good baby so they weren't prepared the second time with me, she says, even *with* the set of instructions from the hospital, those medical people don't always think about the difficulties involved with treatment in the home.

Everything had to be timed just right, the atropine drops before and after each feeding, the bottle heated to an exact temperature no more no less, they showed her in Recovery how to hold it a certain way and the baby too at just the right angle prior to inserting the nipple but everything took so long, step by step, even when she got it right, she'd finally finish and do the cleaning up and it was time to start the whole thing over.

There had to be a precise interval between feedings. She was under strict instructions.

And Daddy tried so hard, you have to give the man his due, he'd warned her before the wedding ceremony there were things he simply didn't have the constitution for, most men don't, he'd never changed a diaper in all the years with Mia after they had Thomas, he said it made him gag uncontrollably.

He gave it his best though, it was touching sometimes really, he bought her the loveliest nursing gown, lace, for her first day home from the hospital, she came down to the living room babe in arms and there he was all dressed up in his smoking jacket and slippers, he must have wanted to make a real occasion of it.

Well, you can imagine.

He got the bottle from the kitchen stove and she administered it, they did all the right things, she was sitting on the velvet loveseat, his grandmother's, remember how they had it there against the front window facing the street? That must have been right after they got it re-covered the first time.

Not for long. So to speak.

They couldn't have been more than halfway through the feeding and whoop! There she went.

To use an expression.

All over everything, the sofa, the good Persian carpet, there were times they even had to scrub the walls afterward.

Victor was very calm, he just put down his pipe and went to the hall closet and got his overcoat and hat, he said, "That's it for me, Lillian."

Well, you go through things with a child, you survive, they promised to operate if it didn't resolve itself by six months, you learn to wait things out, they don't like to put a newborn under the knife right away.

She has to laugh at how innocent they were, she and Victor, they wanted everything to go right, parents always do, but you never know with a child, it's the same in all families, each one's different, Margaret did things right on schedule, crawling, walking, her children were all good walkers really, even you, she says, you tried to keep up.

She says there was a time they were afraid I'd never walk at all.

She remembers how I'd lie on the floor for hours sucking that finger of mine, staring up at the ceiling, it was hard to get you interested in things, she says, too sick maybe, the intellectual child it turns out, you were probably thinking.

They laughed at how I made my way around a room, one hand dragging over the wall and the furniture, they thought it was just my way of doing things, always a different approach, the other hand was in my mouth of course.

They didn't consider what a tiny place it was, you remember, she says, that house was so crowded, all the antiques, the Victorian armchairs, the loveseat, the mahogany bookshelves, not to mention the normal things every family has, she had to wash and wax the kitchen floor before she left for the hospital, she was so pregnant with Clare she could barely bend over but the cleaning had to get done, she wouldn't be back for ten days, that was the custom back then, she moved whatever she could into the next room, the dinette set, the extra chairs, pushed the dough tray and the heavy things against the wall, she was on her knees for half an hour, bucket and mops stranded beside the back door, the wax hadn't even begun to dry when she looked up.

There you were, she says, the baby, standing at the opposite end of the kitchen by the dining room entrance clutching the doorjamb for support that way you always did, and then all of a sudden you let go, you weren't holding on to anything, one foot down then the other, you started walking right out onto the wet kitchen floor, your first steps by yourself, who would have believed it? They laughed for days afterward, all those months of hugging the walls just waiting for someone to clear a space, it had never occurred to them.

She had to act fast to save her floor of course, she called out, "No, no, Wendy, stop! Mama will come get you!" Then she went out the back door, around the house, and in through the front.

She was in Delivery the next day, it was that close, Daddy looked after Margaret and me, he even got us up and dressed in the mornings, of course that woman came to help, you remember, she says, what's-her-name, the oft-quoted Mrs. Rivers, she stayed before with Margaret when you were born, Victor drove all the way out to that farm to get her, both you girls loved her so, it wasn't her fault what happened, people didn't always understand the causes of things back then, she was very experienced, an older woman, from that *good* kind of farm people.

Well, they know things today, infant diarrhea, no one even used the term in those days, she's glad really, babies used to die from it, very frightening for the parents, Victor didn't tell her at the hospital, they kept her there for ten days, that's the way it was done back then, he must have been afraid the worry would slow her recuperation but really it was worse coming home to it, a second trauma after the natural trauma of birth, you'd have to experience it yourself to understand what it was like for her, she could hardly bear to look, she says I wasn't the kind of toddler who could afford to lose that kind of weight.

It was sad too, they had to teach me how to walk all over again, I'd forgotten how, Daddy would take my hand, she says, and try to coax me a few steps at a time across the bedroom floor.

Teeter-totter
Seesaw
Getting up
& down
makes sounds

The higher the window
the lower down
the ground

Salt Land

When we were little Clare and I shared an imaginary kingdom called Salt Land. So Margaret made up her own world, Kinston, and drew a map of wavy rivers and mountain ranges with her fountain pen. She produced a document listing the rules, scrolled it up, and tied it with a red ribbon. No inhabitant of Kinston could make contact with Earth except in an emergency. They were permitted only to hover some feet above its surface. The sole exception cited was Margaret, their missionary to the planet, who was allowed to touch down.

Salt Land lacked the intricacy. Its only drama involved a red plastic telephone on which Clare and I made calls to inquire whether our enemy, Mr. Kraft from Pepper Land, was in or out of his mind.

My own private game was called Being Somebody. It required sitting on the front steps by myself and making up a story in my head.

Margaret wanted to be a real missionary when she grew up. She put on the black cassock from her Junior Choir robes and conducted services in her room. She practiced being perfect, trying to go the whole day from the moment she got out of bed, but Daddy always ruined it with a scolding. She burst into tears: "Now I have to start all over again!"

She developed a slight stutter.

She sent Adlai a nickel for his campaign with a note about the hole in his shoe. Mother gave it to our neighbor, who published it in his column in the weekly newspaper. At Christmas he printed letters to Santa by each of us—Margaret asked only for something for the children in poor families.

She fought to protect Clare and me at the pool at Oak Street Park when an older boy tried to dunk our heads. She kicked and splashed and scratched until he backed off. He was from the only Negro family in town, the one dark face in a sea of fair flesh.

The first week after we moved to North Carolina Margaret drank from the fountain labeled COLORED in the lobby of the movie theater, and Mother and Daddy had to take her aside for quick instruction in the local customs. We rented a house from another professor who was on sabbatical with his family for a year while Daddy looked for something to buy. The three of us slept in the attic. Every morning Daddy rapped on the trapdoor to wake us. His head came up through a hole in the floor.

Margaret had a Negro doll she kept out on her shelf even after she stopped playing with dolls. The chocolate skin had peeled on one arm to reveal white underneath, so she patched it with a flesh-colored bandage. She had a pen pal Mother found for her in the back pages of the *Forward*—Sister Jeanne, a nun with the Episcopal mission in Haiti.

We were High Church, but St. Ann's, the parish we joined after Daddy bought our first house among the bankers and tobacco executives in the section of town called the Valley, wasn't. Many of the congregants had been Baptists before their fortunes rose. Nonetheless Mother continued to cross herself when the priest gave the Absolution and to genuflect deeply when the Cross passed by during the Processional. The three of us dipped our heads after her, meek as shorebirds, trying to distinguish ourselves as little as possible from our unbowed neighbors in the other pews.

We called our priest "Father" even though Southerners said "Reverend" for all men of the cloth no matter what denomination or else plain "Mister." Father Jones at St. Ann's became Father Bill when he got to be like an old friend of the family after a few months. Mother wanted Father Bill to hear Confession from each of us in preparation for the Confirmation ceremony when we turned thirteen—after all, little Catholic girls do it every week. He finally found the form in the Church of England prayer book and met with us in succeeding years in his parish study. Margaret suffered through an agony of silence trying to think of a sin till he forgave her anyway, stressing "those things we ought to have done" rather than those we ought not. When it was her turn, Clare burst into tears at the start, and Father Bill had to spend the whole session calming her down. I tried preparing a list beforehand for mine, but it got out of hand until I figured out that all the sins in the world really fit under one category—lying.

Every summer the three of us spent two weeks at the Diocesan camp, Camp Venite, in the foothills of the Smoky Mountains. Margaret graduated over time from camper to counselor to staff member and finally camp secretary, a position she held till the summer she graduated from college and got married. As lowly campers Clare and I caught glimpses of her with the other staffers out on the smoky staff dining porch, where laughter erupted over some sophisticated joke, or on the Residence veranda in one of the big old platform rockers, slapping at bugs and having deep conversations.

Venite was like another world—released from the laws of gravity. Margaret smoked. The camp director T.J. taught her to drive the camp station wagon so she could help out with errands. She learned the banjo and sang harmony with a boy named Tad, short for Tadpole, on numbers like "Wildwood Flower" and "Banks of the Ohio." The most popular member on the staff was Blue, the camp dishwasher. For most of them, he was their first black friend. The times were changing, Margaret and Tad sang. When a young deacon—one of Margaret's many admirers—took me along for the ride to put a homesick girl from my cabin on the bus, he explained *Brown vs. Board of Education* to the two of us. I repeated his story for my parents when I got home, and Mother asked, "Does this mean you're an Integrationist?" I said I guessed it did.

Creeping & Crawling

"I'm sorry, I'm sorry, I'm sorry. Oh, I'm so sorry."

"Stop it, Lillian!"

"Sorry."

"Shut up! You hear me? You'll make yourself silly, is that what you want? You want the girls to see this, you want the neighbors coming over? You think you can frighten me don't you, with your fainting and your cheap hysterics. You think you can wriggle out of everything. Move, move! Get out of my way I said, I'm going upstairs."

She creeps across the room. She shows us: "creeping across the room."
The way slope-headed primates stalk a jungle landscape.
The sloth at the zoo.
She pulls down her mouth at one corner and lets her jaw hang. Turns her face so we can see. Eyes wide and rolling—one snap and they could furl up into the sockets, her head could snap back.
What does she mean?
She's acting out what's happening, it's a demonstration. How the human body functions in distress.
Slowing her moves to illustrate. One foot set down. Then the other.
Someone needs to be rescued. This is how to recognize the signs.
But no one can move in that atmosphere, it's hopeless as a dream. Bar by bar the giant sloth makes its way as the children watch. Strapped to their high chairs. Paralyzed to the eyes. No hands to reach out to her, no hearts.

Children Don't Remember

They say the average adult smiles only four times a day while the average child smiles four hundred times, there was a study, she must have read about it at the hairdresser's, it's a good idea, she tries to remind herself every day now, it's good to get in some practice, even when there's no one else there she'll walk around the house sometimes with a smile on her face.

You have to think about the good things in life, remember the jolly times, cheer yourself up, smile whether you feel like it or not.

She doesn't get depressed, *depression*'s not a word she'd ever use about herself, it's not in her vocabulary really, you see enough sour old ladies in church, the only time she had depression was when we were all toddlers at the same time, the three of us running around, they gave her something for the nervousness.

Her own father was depressed when she was growing up, she realizes it now looking back, after he lost his job and then the accident, falling off that ladder, breaking his leg, he was too discouraged to look for work after that, her mother begged him, what good would it have done though, it was the Depression.

Her poor mother, such a hard life, then dead at fifty from a heart attack, it was a shock coming home from college for the funeral, finding out her father was pulling up stakes and moving back to Illinois to live with his sisters, losing her home and her mother in one fell swoop.

Well, it's never easy, it wasn't easy for the three of you girls growing up the way you did, she says, she knew that, she saw what it was like, it's hard for a mother to have to watch, children will forget, we know that now, studies have shown, they don't remember accurately, it's probably better for everyone in the long run actually.

You had a perfectly normal childhood, she says, she has pictures of us smiling.

Shadow

From the time she could walk, Clare was at my heels. Running out from under the swing set, chubby legs churning, diaper dragging. Bawling, "Wait for me!" Margaret wrote a poem called "Wendy's Shadow," with Daddy's help, for Clare's sixth birthday.

> Nothing you could ever do
> Would make me change my "I love you,"
> Sister of Wendy.

It was Clare who showed me, when we were seven and eight, how to masturbate along the edge of the mattress. We shared one room or another from the time Clare moved into the nursery till her freshman year of high school when Margaret left for college. We swore by the same early memories—the sound of reindeer hoofs scrambling for a hold on the icy shingles over our heads, the crack of a bat splitting the summer night and a roar going up from the crowd at Oak Street Park in the spotlit corner of the playground where the town ended in cornfields.

Then we moved to North Carolina, and I met Prissy. We became best friends because of a fight in the fourth grade. Prissy called Donna's mother a bitch. Shock waves traveled across the playground. Girls met in groups, sides were chosen. My mother had taught me to be friends with everyone. Who could tell what might happen in the years after fourth grade, whose friendship you might need? I was relatively new, I still talked like a Yankee. I wanted to please everyone. Most of all, though, I wanted to please Prissy. I chose Prissy. My fate was sealed through the end of high school.

She was right, anyway. Donna's mother was a bitch.

My parents were dubious about our friendship—the long phone calls, the intense exchange of intimacies outside the family. On the few occasions Prissy spent the night with me, we had to tiptoe or Daddy said we kept him up all night and ruined his day the next day. At the dinner table he told long stories like the one about the prisoners who were lifers and memorized their jokes and called them out by number in the prison dining hall. Prissy looked mystified when he paused for her response.

It was better to stay at Prissy's house. We took a big old blanket from her mother's linen closet and went outside at three AM and spread it in the middle of the street. Then one of us lay down on it and the other rolled her up inside. When the rare car turned onto Prissy's road, there were screams of hilarity, frantic pushing and shoving as the girl inside the blanket tried to stand up and walk. Prissy's mother woke up and shouted to us from the front porch, then went grumbling back to bed.

My mother said those other friends will leave you but you always have your sister—as if I might forget the shape in the other bed, whose breathing I listened for. Prissy and I tried pairing Clare with Prissy's sister Dooley, but it didn't take. Dooley was two grades behind Clare, they had nothing in common. They trailed along after us on our various excursions, inevitably falling behind, drifting apart. But Clare was still the one I came home to, the one I sat opposite night after night and tried to entertain, like the prisoners in Daddy's story, grimacing in the fun-house mirrors of the knives and spoons, kicking her under the dining room table so she had to concentrate on keeping a straight face while the grownups' arguing held center stage. Margaret, if she was home, warned us, "Control yourselves, girls."

I won the Miss Junior High pageant at Venite one year, a stick figure in heels and a bikini, and Clare won it the next. The judges were counselors and priests. They said they loved the poem I recited, "Black Days, White Nights," an original composition about playing the piano, which Daddy had helped me write. The pounding rhythms and relentless alliteration owed something to Poe and something to "The Highwayman." A handsome, redheaded deacon predicted they would hear from me one day.

He leaned inside the driver's window to congratulate our parents when they came to pick us up at the end of the camp session. In the back seat Clare twirled around her wrist my tinsel crown, which I'd given her permission to hold for some of the ride home.

The redheaded deacon indicated Clare. "That's the one you should watch," he said. "She's going to be your real beauty."

The car, idling, made the temperature even hotter. Our bare legs stuck to the vinyl upholstery. I was bleeding into the pad my cabin counselor had shown me how to use that very week.

My days in a child's body were coming to an end—the spread of my nose increasing, pustules hardening under the skin. I'd popped my first pimple only months before in the front hall mirror, my mother's pride with the scalloped, rococo edge. I squinted. No wonder Daddy scolded me about my poor powers of observation. I was going to need glasses.

Clare had fair skin, the kind that would never blemish. Her thick hair was dark and shiny, it was gold and fine on her arms and legs. Long legs. Her breasts had already begun. It was easy to see how things would turn out. My shadow was going to eclipse me.

Emergency

He was mowing the lawn on the Fourth of July. He wore madras bermuda shorts, a white sport shirt, and a pair of canvas shoes that Mother hated him in.

A stick flew up and slashed him across the knee, viciously.

We were in the house when we heard him yell because no one was ever out there helping him with things, he said we wouldn't care if the whole place fell down around our ankles.

Blood dripped down his leg. He had to drive himself in to Emergency. If he stopped breathing someday, he'd have to give himself artificial respiration.

Once he tried to start a fire in the fireplace but the logs we'd brought in for him from the wood pile were damp, he said we must have taken them from the top. Lillian might have reminded him to order more kindling but that would be asking her to think.

He went into the utility closet and brought back the can of lighter fluid that he used for the charcoal grill. He squirted it in the fireplace and then threw in the match.

Fire leapt up following the arc of the liquid, a hoop of flame from the hearth to the can. The can was on fire.

He shouted, "Move! Move! Out of my way!" He held the flaming can at arm's length and followed it through the family room into the laundry room and out the back door onto the patio.

He dropped it on the flagstones and yelled for the garden hose.

Then he had to yell for another girl to run to the side of the house and turn on the damn spigot.

We all might have been killed if he hadn't kept his wits about him.

He was backing us down the driveway onto our road when he told everyone to shut up, just for one minute, could we? Shut the hell up.

He lowered his chin and waited to let a long belch make its way through his body.

He must have passed out there for a second, he said.

Imagine what would happen to all of us if he were to pass out behind the wheel.

Once upon a time a long long time ago, in Iowa, he parked on a steeply graded incline. The three of us were in the back. Mother in the passenger seat, staring out the windshield. He got out to go up to a house and see some people.

We started to roll. We were slipping away, tires peeling back the adhesive of the gravel drive.

He was almost to the front door, about to ring the bell.

Mother didn't move. Eyes forward.

He turned around and saw us.

He raced back, stuck his arm through the window and yanked the emergency brake.

Fool!

She probably didn't even know where the damn thing *was*.

That was the sound of emergency—like Velcro slowly tearing.

Mother, her back against the slippery surface, sliding down the white icebox and slumping to the linoleum. Daddy slamming out the kitchen door.

Something like that.

When she fed Clare sleeping pills instead of aspirin one summer, they had to walk Clare up and down the bedroom we shared to keep her awake through the night. It was an unfamiliar medicine cabinet in one of those faculty homes we rented in Madison, it wasn't her fault. Later Daddy took me for a walk outside on the sidewalk, back and forth in front of the house, to calm me.

It was wiser to leave medical things to him in the first place. He was the one who held my hand and walked beside the gurney when they wheeled me down to the operating room for my tonsillectomy when I was three. Mother couldn't. She never could stand to witness the suffering of children, she says, it's just something about her.

When we got sick, it was Daddy who scolded us into bed, took our temperature and called the doctor, drove us to the appointment even if he had to cancel class to do it. In the meantime there was usually something he could scare up from his medicine cabinet to tide the patient over.

He made broth and brought a cup upstairs, fussing in the cupboards to find the one or two crumbled bouillon cubes—Mother never remembered to put them on the list for him when he did her grocery shopping.

She filled in for him only when someone had to throw up in the middle of the night—he must have felt the same way he did about changing diapers. She left their bed at the first sounds of commotion to find whichever girl it was bent in misery over the toilet bowl, barely aware her mother had slipped up from behind until she felt the touch of a hand against her forehead.

When the doctors had to cut Daddy open the first time, for his gallbladder, Mother sent us off to grade school with a warning.

"Remember, girls—at eleven o'clock your father goes under the knife."

That was our second year in North Carolina. It was a serious operation back then. We were living in the gray prefab, before it got too small. It was the second house after the second turn-off into the Valley. They made it a joke: the second marriage in the second house inside the second gate.

I got hepatitis.

I lay propped on the sofa in front of the picture window, TV at the far end. Quiz shows in the morning, soap operas in the afternoon. Because of my special circumstances, I was also allowed a stack of comic books brought over by a family friend.

I heard Daddy in the study on the phone. He had a headache and a bellyache, he just didn't feel that well, he'd canceled his morning class.

There was a set of French doors hung with a blue curtain between the study and the living room. He shoved the chair back and something fell down.

He pushed open the doors. He was in blue pajamas and his bare feet. I had on knee socks and a robe over my nightgown, the checkered afghan from his grandmother covering my knees.

He crossed the living room and on through the dining room out to the kitchen, padding across the linoleum. There was a disturbing sound.

I found him at the sink throwing up. There may even have been some blood. He remembered it vividly. How I said, "You belong in a hospital!"—it sounded like a line from one of my soap operas. How the McAfees next door loaded him into their station wagon and delivered him to the door of Emergency.

It was serious. The ileum was inflamed and they had to take out a sizable portion of intestine. Then he developed endocarditis—he joked it was his only sympathetic link to President Eisenhower. For two weeks they treated him intravenously, hooked up to God knows what kind of machines, he said.

When he came home, he tottered. He couldn't seem to recover his spirits. Nights were the worst. He roamed the house. Made himself tea. Wrote down some lines for a poem on the back of a phone bill. Sometimes he has to use whichever bathroom's nearest—his own, next to the study, the one in their bedroom, the one my sisters and I use in the middle of the upstairs hall. He doesn't always flush, he can't be expected to remember. Or else he has to save the evidence to examine in the daylight when he's clearheaded so he can report back to the doctor. Consistency, color, any traces of blood. We stumble in on it in the morning.

We were lucky. Wherever you lived in the Valley, you were surrounded by doctors. Whenever Mother saw a group of them out on the golf course, she always remarked on the sacrifices they had to make for their profession—leaving their beds and wives at any hour to snatch someone from the jaws of death.

When Daddy bought the house on Darby Road in 1959, we inherited a retired radiologist on the left and a dermatologist across the street. If Daddy had a pain in the night or Mother thought her heart was beating too fast, they called the radiologist and he came over in his robe and overcoat with his black bag. He never minded. He took blood pressure, then they had a nightcap of brandy to settle everyone down.

He was the one who decided, toward the end, whether or not it was necessary to call the ambulance.

It pulled in quietly, rolling over the stones of our driveway. The paramedics loaded my father in, and the radiologist arranged to follow them to the hospital with Mother in his sedan. I rode in the front of the ambulance next to the driver. We skimmed the black streets almost without a ripple. Fast but not too fast. Lights but no siren. The man knew how to steer through an emergency.

A Fight Then a Rescue

Sometimes a fight ends in a rescue. Mother, her face smeared and blubbery, collapses on the stairs. She moans and shakes her head from side to side.

"Stop it, Lillian, stop it!" He bends down over her. "You're making yourself hysterical." He takes her face between his hands. He slaps at her cheeks, first one then the other, lightly, professionally. She pulls away, still moaning. She drags herself up the few remaining steps to the upper floor, then, stumbling and crawling, like a wounded animal limping and recovering, she makes off down the hall to their bedroom. He dogs her heels, into the bedroom and the adjoining bath beyond.

He overtakes her at the medicine cabinet. She wrenches open the door and begins to claw and plunder, raking the content of the shelves, reaching for everything in sight: bottles of aspirin, stomach medicine, a box of bandages.

The serious, prescription drugs, he keeps separate in his own bathroom downstairs.

He grabs her arms. He almost pins her—leading her sobbing back into the bedroom and over to the bed.

Their door closes. Sobbing behind. His voice. More sobbing. Softer. Now low talk.

In the morning, before he drives her to work, he prepares her tray of orange juice, toast, and coffee as usual. Before carrying it up with the newspaper, he pauses at the kitchen door and says, "Try to be especially nice to your mother today, girls, won't you?"

The Boys

They embraced and kissed each other on the lips like European men. When Uncle Frank came through the airport gate, he was wearing a red and black flannel shirt and no tie. Mother eyed the costume. Margaret and Clare and I jumped up and down to reach his height. His cheek was whiskery with salt-and-pepper stubble even though it was only midday. We hung on him on either side all the way to the parking lot.

He and Daddy talked through the drive home, then in the study for the rest of the afternoon, Daddy in the captain's chair with his pipe and Uncle Frank on a straight chair brought down from the dining room for his back. They told stories from the past, growing up at their grandparents' house on a leafy boulevard in St. Louis at the beginning of the century. Mama wasn't suited to domestic life so Dad arranged for permanent lodgings for the two parents at the old downtown hotel, and they went over to Nana's for meals with the boys. Someday Daddy and Frank were going to write a book collecting all the stories about the family's beloved cook Barbara, who was also a medium and often spoke, in her mangled mixture of German and English, through her familiar spirits Blue Flower and Red Feather, former American Indians. When Frank dated a Mexican-American girl, Barbara passed on the disapproval of those on the Other Side. "Ve don't need that in our family," she said, laying a finger against the side of her nose as she paused to consider. "Our family is bad enough as it is."

There were boxes and boxes in Daddy's study closet and in Frank's attic in Chicago, full of their notes, their correspondence over the years, as well as letters and telegrams from Dad after the boys left home, recalling the latest "Barbarism."

Our dinner table was transformed when Uncle Frank came to visit. He didn't bow his head or cross himself at the end of the Blessing— he said he was an atheist. Sometimes he laughed so hard, Clare and Margaret and I sprang up and rushed around the table to hold him in his chair: was it in Bristol or somewhere in Wales, Daddy was saying, the inn where the decrepit butler had to climb five flights to answer another of Mama's summonses and spying her snow white pompadour at the top of the stairs growled: "And what would you be wantin', *George Washington.*"

They were teenagers when Mama took them on the Grand Tour of Europe and the British Isles. Dad stayed home to run the family dry goods business. They worked out a shorthand for telegrams to let him know all was well, but halfway through the journey he cabled, "Have lost the code. Stop. Call home." Whatever else you said about Mama, her sons agreed, she had a sense of fun. She was passionate about Teddy Roosevelt and the St. Louis Browns. She took the boys out of school to see the Browns play.

Frank visited North Carolina every few years, usually when he could invent a business trip, but he only brought his whole family with him once, four years after we'd moved there. Mother and Aunt Harriet conferred in the kitchen while the five of us girls played Hearts until no one could stand another game. Hadley and Kate mocked our new accents, testing us on *downtown* and *high tide*. When it snowed, we piled on the sled three at a time so one girl went flying into the soft yard when we crashed at the end of the long driveway.

They were our only relatives except for our half brother Thomas, whom we had never seen. When he showed up suddenly at our house and stayed for a week he proved to be so ordinary it seemed like a miracle. He teased our friends. He took the three of us on a tour of the tobacco factory, where my parents had never taken us, and asked the pretty tour guide for a date. When he left, it was as if he disappeared into the mists again. He lived in California with his mother and stepfather and was going back there to finish college and become a sportswriter—a career my father could never have imagined a son of his pursuing.

We didn't see Hadley and Kate again till we were practically adults, at Margaret's first wedding. After the ceremony all but the honeymoon couple went down to South Carolina to the cottage Daddy had put himself deep in debt to buy at "the shore"—he and Uncle Frank called it that from their boyhood summers on Block Island. They spoke of *bathing* in the ocean. They waded out to their navels then splashed themselves under the arms and a little across the torso before plunging in. Daddy said nothing helps like the salt water.

Hadley's hair had grown down to her waist. She sat on the beach blanket and played protest songs on the guitar. Mother said how you dress is your own business but other people have to look at you. She didn't want Daddy to grow a beard the way Frank did after he retired, she thought it made old men look their age.

Frank always planned to stop shaving for good the first morning he didn't have to go to the office. It was all part of the pose, Mother said, even if it *was* true. The rebel in the business suit. That kind of thing is hard on wives. When Frank traveled for his job, he removed all the Gideon Bibles from the hotel rooms he stayed in and replaced them with Latin textbooks.

Well, Mother said, you have to admit you don't find that combination of scholar and businessman in the world today. He and Victor divided the world along the Pyrenees when they were boys—Frank took everything to the south. He was desperate to get to Spain for the war, but his paper sent someone else. After that he gave up on journalism, put his novel in a drawer, and called Dad's friend at J. Walter Thompson. He still translated and wrote poems, mostly limericks and haiku but some were serious—in a different league from his brother, though, Daddy would point out, his long career of published articles and translations, his two books of poetry, one the winning volume in a statewide competition. He and Frank queried each other back and forth over questions of word derivation and told stories on the characters in the history books.

Mother said the family rumors that Frank was working for the CIA at some point were true, but that was the *old* CIA—it was different in those days. They sent Frank and his family all over the globe. His family got a real education with all that travel, that's one thing you had to say for Frank. Hadley was born in Colombia. If her father wanted to look like Hemingway in his retirement, if he wanted to spend all that money to build himself a house in Mexico when they only stayed there half the year, who could deny him?

He did look like Hemingway, a cheerful Hemingway, and like Daddy too. They were never closer to anyone than to each other—exchanging letters every week, phone calls every month or two at a time when long distance was considered a luxury by most people. Mother said it was almost unnatural.

The older they got, the more they resembled each other, like two versions of the same man. North and South. Grant and Lee, when they fought the Civil War on their grandparents' lawn, Daddy already pledged to the old Southern gentleman. That was still the last great war when they were boys. Both gray-haired now, they posed on the steps of our house with their arms around each other's shoulders—the same scimitar mouth, the high intelligent forehead. Their blue eyes put a light in their faces that made them look forever young and expectant.

Tongue Out

She's got him bolloxed. He's baffled. Balked at every turn. Trying to bulldoze him like that again with her stiff-necked silence. Standing beside the table—an armload of dishes.

Insisting she doesn't know what she's supposed to be sorry for!

He pushes back his plate. Gets up. Stomps off a few paces then turns on his heel. Back, try again. But she won't budge. His frame shudders with fury, like a dog shaking off water. A boxer psyching himself in his corner between rounds.

Halt, march, halt. Seven steps from the dining room to the front hall. He stands there between the flights of stairs, one up, one down. Sticks his tongue out.

Girlfriends

Prissy was a cool blonde. Her hair was almost white on top, darkening to a kind of no-color underneath. Her skin was a smooth tallow, her clear gray eyes made a steady appraisal of the things and people around her.

Adults never liked this. In high school a teacher warned me, "Don't get hard like Prissy."

Her name was a common one for little girls in the South but exotic to me: bestowed some weekend morning in the living room of a ranch-style house near a golf course by a young matron lazing like a cat on her sofa, one hand holding a Bloody Mary or a tall glass of iced tea. So much ice has melted in the tepid Southern morning that the drink threatens to spill over as she makes a pretense of rising to look over the rim of the glass when her golden preschooler marches in and twirls before her mother in a new dress stiff with crinolines.

"Well, looky-here," the mother says, watching her tallow-dipped child. "If it isn't Miss Priss." Her voice is honey and vinegar, her own hair is harshly peroxided.

Most girls lose the nickname as they grow up or it stays at home, but with Prissy it stuck, it worked. It made a space around her that kept her a little apart, like the cool currents stirred by a paper fan or a starched petticoat you can twirl in.

In the fifth grade we had a club called The Big Five. The other members were Randall, Rusty, and Clarence. They were the smart boys, our best friends all through school, occasionally our boyfriends. When a whining girl named Patsy asked to be in our club, we voted unanimously no. We didn't want to change our name. The teacher, Mrs. Brighton, found out and kept us in for recess. "No one's big enough," she lectured us, "to call themselves The Big Five."

Prissy pointed out it was in the fourth-grade reading book—Alice and Jerry and some other people, they had a club named The Big Five. But Mrs. Brighton didn't appreciate the enlightenment. She made Prissy stay after school.

Prissy's father died the night before school started in the sixth grade. He came home from his job as a chemist at the tobacco factory and lay down on the sofa to take a nap and never got up. I was reading *Little Women* when Prissy called me—Beth was dying in her sister's arms and I was sorry to be interrupted. I didn't know what to do. My parents offered to drive me over to Prissy's house, but I was afraid. For years after that, Prissy thought Donna's mother, who was their neighbor, kept me from her.

The next day at school I didn't know what to say. Prissy put her arm around my shoulder and walked me up the stairs to find our new classroom and teacher.

There were rumors about Prissy's mother and other men after her husband died. She was only thirty. I thought she was like a movie star—rising at noon on Saturdays to show up in her kimono in the kitchen, where Prissy and I were drinking Kool-Aid after our morning bike ride. She and Prissy exchanged challenging remarks and let them drop. Once she let me taste her martini.

Eighth grade was our wildest year. Everyone in our class pulled together to rebel. We met in the park after school to smoke. At slumber parties the girls strolled the neighborhood arm in arm after midnight looking for the boys. Our teacher was Mrs. Mordred, a horsey blonde with buck teeth who wanted to be like a friend. We hung her in effigy the second week, her raincoat tied with a jump rope to the rafter of lights, rubber boots dangling below the hem. The principal was summoned. He asked the ringleaders to stand so he wouldn't have to punish the whole class. The whole class stood up.

Mordred was wild for Nixon. She gave me the Kennedy side of the hall bulletin board and teased me in class with breathy imitations of Jackie's voice. She liked to discuss the extensive gun collection she and her husband kept.

I brought home B's instead of A's on my report card. Mordred called my parents and said Prissy and I were the class leaders in troublemaking, which was more than we could have hoped for. She told them I smoked, which I denied. Daddy wanted to make an appointment for me to see their friend Tilly von Reichman, but I cried and said I wasn't crazy.

Prissy fell in love with Johnny Pickett, the handsomest boy in the two eighth grade classes. They made a duet of silver blond perfection. I had a crush on the glamorous music teacher, Mrs. Poe, who taught the other eighth grade class and who was kind to me. She used endearments like *Dear* and *Little One*. She had a laugh that bubbled up from high C, then went down to G, then a long D. I hung around after music period to listen while she practiced at the piano, her long arms sweeping up and down the keyboard, the crashing chords of Rachmaninoff striking the rafters of the old auditorium like brass. She played some of her own compositions too—I'd never met anyone who wrote her own music. Songs without words, songs she sang for me. A piece set to the epigraph of *The Great Gatsby*:

Then wear the gold hat if that will move her.
If you can bounce high, bounce for her too,
Till she cry "Lover, gold-hatted, high-bouncing lover,
I must have you."

Her husband was the high-hatted golden lover—a doctor as handsome as Mrs. Poe was beautiful. We daydreamed in whispers about their life together. Maybe she taught him songs on the ukulele, as she did us, campfire relics from a romantic past we could only imagine: "King Edward was noble, King Edward was great, but 'twas love that caused him to abdicate."

I was mystified by Prissy's new state. I still had two years to go before I met Patrick in high school. No one like Johnny would ever choose me. I cultivated a few of my more peripheral friendships to fill in the times I was left alone. A girl named Kathy had a crush on a different teacher, and we plotted together how to engineer accidental encounters with the objects of our affection.

When school ended in June, I missed the bus deliberately and cornered Mrs. Poe outside the teacher's lounge. I threw myself at her and cried because I'd never see her again—except maybe at St. Ann's, where she put in the rarest of appearances. That summer we wrote a hymn together, and the Junior Choir sang it on Christmas. Mrs. Poe sent me a present, a record of Rachmaninoff's Third Piano Concerto that I played so many times I memorized the scratches.

But the day the eighth grade ended, I didn't see any future at all. Mrs. Poe gave me a ride home in her husband's Jaguar. She stopped at the corner grocery store and bought us ice cold Cokes to calm me down. She said I was special and not to forget it in the years ahead. A priest at Venite had told me the same thing when I was ten—taking me aside in private and stroking my back, then sliding his hand down till it slipped inside the band of my underpants. I felt a jolt, as if my soul had leapt out of my body.

For some reason when Mrs. Poe dropped me off, Mother was home from work. She wasn't happy when I came in the kitchen door late.

She disapproved of the vivid young music teacher and her glamorous makeup. She suspected my passion.

Hand On

We were taking naps. He slept on the cot down in his study or else the master bedroom upstairs. He pulled the curtains shut and put a sleep mask over his eyes. I was in my own room at the end of the hall lying on Clare's bed.

I don't know why I didn't lie down on my own bed, maybe it was covered with books and things so there wasn't room. I was masturbating.

I lay on my stomach with the pillow between my legs, I didn't hear the floor creak, I didn't hear a thing.

A hand touched the flat of my back.

I started up.

Nothing, I said, I wasn't doing anything, that wasn't what I was doing.

But he kept it there.

I sank back down.

He rubbed my back and shoulders. I kept my face buried in the sateen bedspread, which was uncomfortable really. He wanted to talk.

He said he felt sorry for me. He was sorry I had to wait for things. He said he only wanted to help me out. Or maybe that was later.

My eyes were shut against the cloth the whole time, I might have been anywhere, I'm not sure what happened when.

Except for this.

There was a boy named Brad from the other eighth grade class. He took a cherry bomb once and went to Mrs. Poe's house and planted it in her bathroom window. He blew up all her bottles of makeup.

I used to sneak over to her house sometimes myself and set up watch hidden in the bushes. Just seeing her car there was reassuring.

Brad wore striped polo shirts that stretched across his chest where the muscles were developing—I remember I was picturing that the moment before my father's hand came down. He was one of those boys who was always getting into trouble.

Fooling Around

Stop fiddling with it.

That's what you get for fooling around.

What are you doing now?

Stop picking at your lips, your fingers.

Can't you keep your hands from your mouth for once?

The reason it's broken is because you kept fiddling with it, and now I'm going to have to pay someone to come all the way out here just to get the damn thing fixed.

Don't you people understand the simple workings of a lock?

You don't know the first thing about the mechanical universe.

You people. Women.

If you don't stop picking at it, you're going to open up the scab again, and then you'll go digging around in there, and it's never going to heal, and you'll end up disfigured for life.

Winners

Mother believed in winning at least one contest per year—she said it looked good on your record. She herself had captured book prizes all through grammar school and had her poems published in the thing they had back then, you know, she says, that was like "My Weekly Reader." Uncle Ed, the nationally syndicated children's columnist, spotted her work and took an interest in her career. If it hadn't been for that she never would have gotten the scholarship to Wisconsin, never signed up for Beginning German and sat in Victor's classroom, screamed at the mouse that ran across the floor, stayed after class and met with him to arrange that he would bring the mousetrap and she the cheese.

She ghostwrote the first Bishop's Cup essay that Margaret won based on Margaret's correspondence with Sister Jeanne. She suggested topics for other contests and sent us to the reference room at the University library, where she was secretary to the head librarian. She composed lines of patriotic verse for the opening of the speech I gave at the North Carolina Jefferson/Jackson Day dinner titled "Why Join a Political Party."

> Slow to anger, quick to heal,
> America rises in concrete and steel.

The auditorium was packed to the rafters with Democrats, but luckily I couldn't see them well enough to be nervous. I spent the prize money on contact lenses. I entered and won the United Nations essay contest as a freshman and then again as a junior so I could visit Kennedy's Eternal Flame when the bus to New York made a stopover in Washington. In the parking lot at Arlington I made a show of rummaging in my purse to find the razor blade I'd stashed there in case I got up the nerve to slit my wrists at the site of my hero's grave, but the history teacher who was chaperoning me saw it and made me throw it away. By the next year the Rules Committee had changed the rules and previous winners couldn't enter. Margaret had won the first year the contest was established.

Clare drew the woman on the matchbook cover to qualify for a correspondence course with a famous artist, but they wrote back saying tracings were ineligible. She cried to Mother and Daddy, protesting that she wasn't smart and didn't want to be. Nevertheless she applied for and won the position of high school columnist for the local paper's Saturday edition, which I'd held for two years and Margaret for two before me.

We branched out into many fields. Margaret had violin lessons,

Clare took flute, and I played the piano. Our parents imagined chamber music in the living room one day. For a while I even went to Saturday classes in music theory taught by a local professor who, when I wrote all my compositions in minor keys, told me "take off the hair shirt." I toyed with the idea of becoming a famous concert pianist but hated to practice. Instead of working on new assignments, I played old pieces I was already good at so when my parents walked by the family room they'd be impressed. I picked out tunes I liked. After seeing Menotti's *The Medium* performed by the NBC Opera on TV, I sat at the piano playing over and over the plaintive line the daughter Monica sang to the grieving Mrs. Nolan, pretending to be the ghost of her dead daughter: "Mother, Mother, are you there? Mother, Mother, are you there?" My father gave me some of his own poems to set to music.

In academics it was Margaret who was the best—honor roll, National Merit Scholar, president of the Episcopal Young Churchmen, secretary of the junior class. She had a long history of good study habits. When the school bus dropped us at the end of the driveway in the afternoons, Margaret went straight up to her room. She removed her skirt and laid it across the bed so it wouldn't wrinkle, opened her books, and arranged things on the desk before sitting down to do the day's homework in her blouse and half slip. Downstairs in the family room Clare and I sprawled in front of the television for the late afternoon soap operas, *The Secret Storm* and *The Edge of Night*.

When Margaret left for college, the family shifted and rearranged itself. Daddy finally got his sabbatical and packed the rest of the family off to Europe. At American Express offices in eight different countries, we picked up Margaret's letters reporting on her grades (A's in everything but Logic) and whom she was dating.

She was always popular. Boys from County fell for Margaret and never forgot her even after she left for college, got pinned, engaged, married when she graduated, and they stayed in town to take over their fathers' gas stations and marry the girls they'd gotten pregnant in high school. She must have inherited some gene from Mother, who had left her own trail of broken hearts behind her in the snows of Albany, boys who swore they'd even marry outside their own churches if she would have them. She'd broken an engagement in Wisconsin to marry Daddy—a boy named Jay who fainted when she told him the news. He was fresh off the farm, training to be a pilot. Later his plane went down. When Margaret broke up with someone, Clare cried and vowed to marry him herself when she was older and rescue him from his grief.

Maiden Voyage

Rouen lies on the Seine. Main cathedral has Gothic styles from 13th, 14th, and 15th centuries. Lovely side chapels like one of St. Cecilia. Statue (modern) of Jeanne d'Arc by Maxim Real del Sartre in ville centre near exact spot where she was burned. Another one in Bonsecours, which is also the Belgian Military Cemetery. Tomb of poet José María de Heredia and his family: "My vagabond soul wandering across the leaves will tremble." (Translation: V.S.)

Clare and I kept journals. We consulted Baedeker. If one of us was too tired and we were getting along, the other one did the work and let her copy it.

Daddy found the birthplace of Pierre Corneille, famous dramatist of Louis XIII's and XIV's time.

Hospital where Flaubert's father worked and son was born. Gustave Flaubert, 1821–1880, great French writer.

He showed us Paris in the snow—l'Arc de Triomphe, largest triumphal arch in the world, and the Louvre, where we stood beneath the Winged Victory and watched a student copy it onto his sketch pad. Her robes look as if they are being blown backward in a wind. (Motion in stone.)

He found the torso of Apollo from Rilke's poem.

We went to the cemetery in Montmartre where Heine, Berlioz, Stendhal, etc. are buried. During the War Daddy's sergeant refused him permission to visit it "just to see a damn bunch of dead Krauts." He bought flowers from a shop nearby and laid them on Heine's grave. Then drove us past the apartment where Heine lived out his exile and died on "his mattress grave" gasping: "Pencil! Paper! Write, write, write, write, write!"

In a café where we had dinner, we ran into Daddy's old Classics instructor from his freshman year at Princeton. He said, "Just like all American professors, always on sabbatical." Afterward we went to an establishment called Caverne des Oubliettes, where a group of young people sang delightful French folk songs. Mother cried. It was also a prison in the 15th-16th centuries.

The night Daddy took Mother to see the Folies-Bergére, Clare and I had sandwiches in the hotel room and did history and English homework. Our paperbacks for school filled a whole suitcase we had to make room for in the crowded luggage compartment of the station wagon. When my copy of *Look Homeward, Angel* went missing, Daddy scoured the bookstores of Paris to find it in the original. It would have made things so much easier, he said, if I'd had my French.

We drove south through the Loire Valley looking for warmth. Stopped at Azay-le-Rideau at a chateau built by Francis I, whose sign is a salamander. The countryside was very picturesque, with vineyards followed by fields dotted with symmetrical rows of haystacks. The smallest hamlet had its church, which is a monumental tribute to the villagers' faith.

At l'Hôtel d' Europe in Poitiers there was no central heating. Clare and I wore robes and socks to bed and huddled under blanket, quilt, and bedspread. The next morning Daddy came in to wake us, and we left early: town still asleep. Inside the car he turned up the heater full blast and we idled beside the Cathedral of St. Pierre, where a magnificent square bell tower next to a round cupola offers an impressive paradox.

In San Sebastián, the tide was gentle but could be heard at night. Young men and boys played soccer on the beach. It was Franco's summer residence. Mother spit behind his statue and said, "Bah, Franco!" When she was sixteen, she'd marched for the Ladies Garment Workers in Albany with her Young People's League from Evangelical and Reform. A shout went up when the men and boys joined their ranks: "The pants are out! The pants are out!" A Catholic boy fell in love with Mother's picture in the newspaper with the caption THE MADONNA OF THE PICKET LINE. She tried to convert for his sake, she even took instruction. But she couldn't accept certain things about the Catholics, like the Intercession of the Virgin.

Along the road to Burgos and Madrid there were towering mountains with snow on them. Daddy said the Rockies were even more spectacular. Someday he might show us the American West, but the real lessons of civilization were here.

We recorded the weather in our journals: "good."

But in the mountains between Zaragoza and Barcelona, there was a sudden sleet storm. The road was winding and precipitous. A lumbering truck appeared from behind a blind curve, and Daddy had to yank the wheel and pull over sharply onto a narrow strip of shoulder to let it pass by. He cursed the other driver, the weather, us. He was the one who bore all the responsibility—the planning, the driving, the entire burden of the journey. It was ever thus. He went on until the accumulation of things left him speechless, and then we rode in a worse silence. From time to time he gave us a blast from the car heater to warm us up, but a mist spread across the inside of the windshield and he had to use his glove to wipe it away, then drive through a tiny hole like that—a hole in his rage.

Between the barbarous rocks and the steep drop below, the road seemed endless. One mistake and we'd go flying off the edge, tumbling from peak to peak until we reached the bottom and settled there, upside down, the family sarcophagus in the undergrowth. No one would ever know.

We recrossed the border and drove back up the map through western France. Then the hydrofoil across the Channel, three days in London, then five in Bristol for the convention that would allow Daddy to write off the trip. There were people he hadn't seen for decades—Kuntz from Yale, Becker from his army days and the department in Wisconsin after that. Professor Alleman, who tutored him in Heidelberg, had snowy tufts of hair growing even from his ears. Dark lapels sprinkled with dandruff.

Clare and I did our homework in the hotel common rooms downstairs. Our writing tables were spindly desks set with blotters, pens in inkwells, hotel stationery and envelopes stacked neatly in the drawers. In the lobby white-haired ladies sat in the stuffed armchairs and settees discussing the health of the Queen. ("Poor dear, she looked pale last night on the telly.") Then they turned to their paperbacks—*The Child Bride of Morleigh Hall* and *Kill Him with a Hammer*. Walls covered in red brocade.

Weather: "sunny patches."

One day Daddy decided to skip the morning sessions and take the car for a tune-up. He made an appointment at a garage in Bath. It wasn't much of a journey, only twenty miles, but he thought he'd make it a day of sightseeing, and he chose me to go with him.

It's likely the Romans were Bath's first discoverers, but according to legend the British swineherd prince Bladud, father of King Lear, founded the town. He was expelled from court as a leper but regained his health by rolling in the warm mud and stagnant mineral waters just like his leprous swine. The Roman name was Aquae Solis or Sulis from Sul, a local deity associated with Minerva. The intricate system of baths is the most important Roman relic in Britain.

We toured the Grand Pump Room and drank from the fountain. Then descended the stone staircase lined with modern busts of famous Romans to the great bath itself—still in a remarkable state of preservation.

At the Abbey Church, Daddy pressed an extra shilling into the warden's palm, and he brought out the processional cross from behind the chancel so we could admire its mother-of-pearl inlays. He left us to stroll the aisles at our own pace. Cruciform building designed in late, not wholly satisfactory example of the Perpendicular style. We stopped to examine memorial slabs set along the windows.

Daddy read aloud: SUFFERED A PREMATURE DEATH BROUGHT ON BY ARDENT AND INTELLECTUAL PURSUITS.

He laughed and read it again.

Get it?

The deceased's name was Manley Powers.

He reintroduced us to the Continent at Dunkerque with the Memorial to the nameless, graveless dead of World War II, then two days later the American Cemetery of the Netherlands, where 1700 soldiers lie quieted under the earth. ("To you from failing hands we lift the torch.") We entered Germany at Aachen (to the Germans; Aix-la-Chapelle to the French). Daddy's first night in "the new Germany" since Repatriation.

Drinks at the hotel bar. At Mother's suggestion I asked permission from the man at the piano and sat down and played the music I'd written back home to Daddy's poem "Mr. Eichmann," but I didn't sing the words.

> Please do not kill Mr. Eichmann,
> although they say he killed me.
> I never knew Mr. Eichmann—
> I was only three.

When I got back to the table, Mother was blotting tears from her eyes. Daddy thought it was interesting that there had never been any women composers—maybe I would be the first.

We sang along the Rhine, or the grownups did, as Daddy drove the winding miles past the illuminated castles. At the Lorelei they sang Schubert's song with Heine's words. Mother knew the German. She understood everything that was said in conversation and read all the newspapers—Daddy could never find enough of them on the newsstands to satisfy her. But she was too shy to speak. God knows why. She had her very own expert—her first and only German professor from Madison—right there to help out if she got into trouble with the verb forms. He'd even said her pronunciation was quite good for someone who'd had to drop out after her third year to get married. But she stubbornly refused to try anything beyond the simplest greetings and phrase book expressions. She sighed at all the beautiful sights of Europe and said, *"Sehr schön!"*

We went to Bad Tölz to meet my godmother and her husband whom I hadn't seen since I was a baby. They were in the States for the War and knew Thomas Wolfe, Sandburg, Frost, Grant Wood. In Vienna because of my musical interests Daddy took me by myself to see Oscar Strauss's "Ein Walzertraum." He hired a carriage for the evening and held my white gloved hand to help me into the seat behind the driver and his gaily plumed horses. At dinner afterward at a restaurant near Kartner Ring, we met the beautiful leading lady. She gave Daddy her calling card. Her dog sat right next to her at his own place at the table—not uncommon among Europeans, Daddy said.

Mother read there was trouble at a Woolworth in Greensboro.

Astronaut Cooper blasted off to circle the earth twenty-two times.

Mother bought dirndls for all three girls, and Daddy got a Tyrolean jacket.

We drove to Italy along a lovely stretch of the Mur. As you get nearer to the border, the Christs along the roadside begin to look more and more uncomfortable.

Bruck-an-der-Mur—Velden—Undine—Venice.

Rain, clearing, rain.

In Padua we viewed Giotto's wonderfully detailed frescoes of Christ and the Virgin.

Drove to the refectory of Santa Maria della Grazie and saw Leonardo da Vinci's *Last Supper* (1494–97). Three groups of four. Christ has just said, "One of you shall betray me." Hands show feeling. Christ's show forgiveness & resignation. Others: nervousness, anger, astonishment.

In Genoa, on our last afternoon, we took a buggy ride (horse was "Nina") then had dinner at a restaurant down the block from hotel. Papers gave bad bulletins on Pope, but our waiter, Gino, said, "Eeh! We make another one!"

51

We left for home on the *Mauretania* the day before Clare's fifteenth birthday.

Gibraltar

The ship docked at Gibraltar for a day. Clare was sick with a high fever—probably something she picked up in Genoa from the food or the dirty streets, Daddy said. She had to spend her birthday below in the cabin berth, pale as death, her eyes sunken. Mother stayed on board with her while Daddy and I went ashore to tour the sights.

All over the peninsula, monkeys skittered across the high, feathery treetops.

Daddy loved monkeys. Ever since he was a boy in St. Louis. He liked their sooty humanoid faces and sad, miming gestures. Whenever he took us to a zoo, the three of us ran ahead first to find the monkey cage. At home, on television, we found a program for him with a chimpanzee in a business suit.

He hired a carriage drawn by a very small donkey, the hybrid of a hybrid, and we followed the hilly road that wound past the Rock of Gibraltar and all along the coastline. Above our heads, fluttering in our hearing, the jabber of the monkeys never stopped. Banter, chatter, chitchat. *Rikk-tikki-tik.* Gibberish filling the air as we bounced along, father-daughter couple steered by a gray-brown miniature donkey.

Man on the Wall

Einstein, Darwin, Marx, Freud, Martin Luther, Copernicus maybe, Descartes, Hegel, Kant. Faces folded in the contours of the gray cortex, waiting to be named.

We met the artist who painted it in a café in Vienna on the

Ringstrasse. Under the dusty chandeliers of the blossoming chestnut trees, sipping *chocolade* and demitasses *mit schlag*. The young man seated at the next table, sketching the scene in front of him on a paper napkin.

Mother nudges us to attention. She thinks it would be nice if Victor said something to the interesting young man.

He's an art student. At the *universitat*. Born just a few kilometers outside the city—yes, of course Daddy knows the village, he remembers passing through during the Occupation. The student admires Daddy's German. Everyone does. In the southern regions, they think he's from the north, and vice versa, but always, without question, a native speaker.

It pleases Daddy, this praise of his endowment, however warranted, however simple the explanation, which he reviews for the student as he would for anyone: a full professor with thirty-five years in the classroom behind him, his degrees, his years of travel, first as a teenager with Mama and Frank then with Mia in Heidelberg at the beginning of their marriage, his years of service in Intelligence.

It pleases both our parents that foreigners so often misjudge us. We must be English, yes? No? Then a nice French family, perhaps. No? No? Surely then at least Canadian. But they can't be serious. Americans? Such well-behaved teenage daughters, American?

We admire the scene on the artist's napkin—the tiny fault lines he's mapped in the façades of the old buildings, the wavy sticks of strolling pedestrians, the wind of the alley into the street. Perhaps we'd like to see more? He has something at a small gallery only blocks away.

Daddy buys a black-and-white lithograph. It's nearly two by two and a half feet in its frame—too large for our station wagon, though Clare and I spend some ten minutes trying to rearrange the luggage. Twenty-two pieces we fit like a puzzle into the rear compartment each time the family packs to leave one hotel for another, one country for the next. Eight countries in four and a half months—no sabbatical from Daddy's worries though, he says, that becomes clearer all the time. He'll have to send the picture by air. More nuisance, more money. If he has a penny left in his pocket by the end of this trip, he'll be lucky. He'll be lucky if he's not arrested when the boat docks in New York and taken off in handcuffs by officials from American Express. Try to do something for this family. Why go to all the trouble and expense of having the car shipped over with us if it's going to be useless at a time like this?

It's not his briefcases that take up so much room, that's for certain—two for his papers, one for his medicine bottles. Those are soft sided, you can wedge things up against them. It's those damn cosmetics cases you women brought, he says, they're so heavy and unyielding.

A few simple purchases he might want to make for himself and no one will accommodate him. Something that could be important to his work, his poetry, the development of his ideas—he's always told us how central these Austro-Hungarian connections are for him. Rilke, Schnitzler, Musil. Try to educate this family. Show us something of the world. Things that have mattered in his life. The sources of Western culture.

The picture's too big at home too, too dominating opposite the three formal photographs of my sisters and me in the upstairs hall where Daddy first tries it. Not subtle enough to replace the graceful black plaster cast of Goethe's death mask on the wall along the stairway. Following the wrought iron railing another flight down, there are three watercolors of Nova Scotia landscapes given to Mother in appreciation by the men in Canadian Studies, where she's served first as secretary and now as Administrative Assistant, writing grants for them. It's the only wall space she's laid claim to, she points out.

Left from the family room, right and left again past Daddy's bathroom toward his study, all the walls are occupied. He couldn't think of sacrificing the magnificent oil of Lee mounted on Traveller or the crossed bayonet and sword from the Franco-Prussian War inherited by his grandfather from a relative who stayed. Mother's clothes closet on the other side eliminates a whole six feet from consideration.

In the study, the secretary and the bookcases reach almost to the ceiling. There's barely space for his photographs—of a sad, mellow Lee retired from Appomattox into the days of his college presidency, the one of Daddy's cigar-smoking father and the two little boys, the autographed one from Thomas Mann.

They decide on my room. Mother's hung some Daumier prints there but they can take those down. It's where Daddy likes to take his afternoon nap. Now he can drift off admiring his new acquisition above the opposite twin bed where Clare used to sleep before Margaret left for college and she inherited the room next door. A year from now all the surfaces—desk, dresser, even the top of the record player—will be covered by my Kennedy memorabilia, photos and black funeral headlines.

The man's brain is boiling out of his skull. His head's giant, swelling into the foreground of the picture. Below it his naked body dwindles away, trailing legs atrophied by perspective, bare muscles and sinews stretched and straining. He floats above skyscrapers, the balloon of his brain's carried him up there along the slant of the buildings that cut across the canvas. He's rising from cavernous depths as sunless as the floors of Wall Street or the area around St. Paul's in London—a twentieth-century hell like the one Daddy teaches about in the second semester of Comp Lit. Six bony fingers signal helplessly from each of his hands.

There's a slit in the lower regions of the mushroom cloud brain, a mouth gap that's vomiting books, a wide and endless stream of books drifting down the oblique steel and concrete corridor to the bottomless streets below. So sick.

One monstrous eye is set into the naked forebrain. Lidless, veined, and bloodshot. Weary with watching from among the gray faces, the great eminences coiled in the bulging gray matter. He wants to weep.

Probably Goethe is sleeping somewhere there, his sockets as bald and emptied of their gaze as the black death mask, shut against more and more light. And Heine too maybe, trying to rise from his deathbed, his voice, his art greedy to go on like the hair and fingernails of a body in the ground. "Pencil! Paper!"

The picture on that wall told everything, it was what everything meant. Europe and why Daddy sacrificed so to take us there, the whole vast canon that was his bequest, his life to ours, in which he must have found the very words he spoke one morning as he rose from my bed:

"He who understands all forgives all."

But who among them said it? Which sage, which gray father? When at last I know all their names, their words, I'll become my father's true daughter and finish the journey he's set me on.

All night the giant head presides over my room, I can almost hear it thinking in the teeming Southern dark that comes right up to the windows, clicking and chiming. And in the gray dawn, it's the first thing I see. It thinks about thoughts, no rest, no end to it—like the oroborus necklace Daddy gave me for my sixteenth birthday. Silver serpent, mouth clamped over tail. He fastened it around my throat the day we boarded the ship and set sail from New York.

Fouling the Nest

Some things it's better not to know.

Not everything was meant to be out in the open, what good does it do, you have to get on with life, it's not healthy to dwell in the past, you have to think about the future, live in the present.

All families have their secrets.

Your father was like that, he clung to the past in everything, he and his brother wrote each other every week of their lives, year in and year out, the constant analysis of everyone in the family long after they were dead, I was always expected to be interested.

All artists are stuck in their childhoods.

I never criticized, I stood behind him, I wouldn't say anything to anyone, I'm not like that, I'd never go outside the family.

You must have picked that up from somewhere, we don't do it in our family, you never learned that in this house.

Always running to some stranger with your troubles

some teacher
some priest
that camp counselor
those other girls.

Just like a baby bird fouling its own nest.

Those other girls will leave you, those other girls will go off and find boyfriends of their own someday.

It's just not in me, I guess, people in my family respected each other, they didn't meddle in one another's lives, I never talked about my family the way your father did, he said my parents were simple people.

You girls don't know what it was like watching you brought up that way, you never realized what I was going through, especially in those early years, children don't, it's a blessing really.

Early on one frosty morn
(every morning)
his frosted eyebrows
his bluebird pajamas
his mind on something else.

On Alert

"Therefore I have ordered that the following steps be taken."
Then a pause.
Mother said, "Oh Victor!"
Daddy said to pipe down. All of us.
For once in our lives?

We were gathered like other families around the television set in the family room. Everyone stopped everything.

The President went on. He'd been aware of the situation for some time.

He brought out charts. He used a pointer—dark blips erupting all across the island nation. A line drawn in the Cuban waters where he was stationing the fleet. All branches of the armed forces to stand by on full alert.

Men came out to the neighborhoods. They measured off quadrants in the backyards and started digging. People went to the grocery stores and cleared the shelves of canned goods, powdered milk, bottled water, toilet paper.

At the high school a memo went out: seniors to the boiler room, juniors like me to the auditorium, Clare and the other sophomores would stand in the hallways where the lockers ran along both walls, freshmen to the lobby, which was glass floor to ceiling on the entrance side. They showed the freshmen how to crouch against the concrete wall opposite and tuck their heads between their knees.

Things went on. People waited as they had during the pause in the President's speech.

The Decorating Committee hung streamers of twisted crepe paper in the gym for the Homecoming dance, and people went ahead and asked out whoever they'd been planning to.

Daddy got the estimate from the surveyor and called the man to cancel the excavation. Mother ran out of some things and had to borrow from the reserve supply: first soup, then the cans of vegetables, Spam for lunch, corned beef hash to fry with eggs when Daddy went to his meeting and there was only herself and the girls to think about for supper.

The light went on in my bedroom. I sat up. Daddy was in the doorway, saying to get dressed.

There was a thin peal of sound coming from the darkness outside the walls of the house.

The skirt and blouse Mother had brought up with the rest of the

58

ironing for me to wear to school were laid out over my desk chair. The closet door slammed and a chair scraped in the next room, where Clare was getting up and dressed too.

Daddy stuck his head in: Better get a move on. They must have sounded the first siren twenty, twenty-five minutes ago.

It stopped.

I snapped the last fastener on my garter and pulled the skirt over my head. I looked around. My World History textbook lay open on the desk where I'd been studying for the quiz—a waste of time now. I went to the closet and got my ukulele. It could be a good thing to have along in the bomb shelter.

Clare and I took our places in the car. Daddy backed out of the driveway onto the dark street. He was tense and muttering over the wheel. Heading out. Past silent neighborhood houses, and then he turned onto the secondary highway that followed the edge of the Valley until it crossed the road to the campus. There was something about a system of tunnels under the University. Margaret would probably be taken there. We would all meet up. He jabbed the air with instructions.

"The radio! Try the radio!" he told Mother. She was such a dumb cluck. First she grabbed the thing for the heater and yanked it all the way up—he had to reach over and seize her fingers and force them over the right place. Then it was: which knob for on and off and which did you use to find the stations?

Idiot! He switched it on himself.

Now the other one—the other one! She fiddled feebly.

It was incomprehensible. A babble. She inched the dial down the band, at his direction, trying to find the crease of sound that would open up and give us news of what was happening.

Cleveland, Pittsburgh, some place in Florida. They overlay each other, they kept interrupting. Countdowns to the Top Ten, deejays breaking in with the call letters of their stations, whooping like loons in the new, hot Sixties manner.

A hundred with-it places battling the air for supremacy. High times everywhere.

"They've jammed the radios," Daddy said under his breath. He nodded. He might have known. He hunched further into the driving. His years of experience in Intelligence were paying off.

He stopped for a red light. The stoplights were still working.

He took a detour through the blocks of faculty homes, rendering our approach to the central campus more clandestine. The houses were dark here too. Maybe the people had gotten out right away.

No more sirens either. They probably would provide a dangerous signal to enemy surveillance.

Daddy found something in Spanish. He'd taken over the operation of the radio himself. His eyebrows worked significantly. His Spanish was second only to his French.

Armamenta.

Americanos.

Kennedy.

A look of recognition crossed Daddy's face. He sat back, his shoulders deflated. His foot eased on the pedal. We reached the traffic island at the entrance to the campus, and he entered the empty lanes, but then he passed right by the turn onto Chapel Drive. The main entrance to the underground tunnels was reputed to be located somewhere down in the chapel crypt.

He passed the exit for the hospital and the one to Alumni Drive. He took us back out the way we'd come in.

He turned the radio off and drove the short route home to the Valley. The houses we passed were still in the dark—our car was a solitary interior, lit by green dials, traveling the empty streets in our state of false alarm.

I returned the ukulele to the closet, pulled on my nightgown, and was rearranging the school clothes over my chair when Mother looked in.

"Did you have to wear those?" she said. "I'd just ironed them so they'd be all fresh and nice for the morning."

Breakfast was a few hours later. Daddy demonstrated for Clare and me the proper method for buttering toast—there's no need to have crumbs on the butter knife when you're finished. He ran water over the can of frozen orange juice, mixed it in the pitcher, and poured it into small glasses.

He loaded Mother's tray and took it up. Then he went down to his study and turned on the stereo to have music while he shaved.

Clare and I went in to tell Mother good-bye. We were brushed and dressed, school books under our arms. She raised herself from the bedclothes so we could reach her cheek to kiss it. We turned to go then, but she stopped us.

"Don't say anything, girls," she said. "About last night. Don't go telling other people."

We waited for the school bus at the end of the driveway. Other kids from the neighborhood used the same stop. The new boy, Patrick, cut through the woods in back of his house and came up the hill. He crossed the street. His hair was still wet from the shower. He wore his shirttail out. The collar was so crisp it might have just come from under the iron. He smelled wonderful.

Poet's Daughter

He cracks the window on the driver's side. He's warned us.

"Remember, I told you, you've been warned. If your mother hadn't kept me waiting we'd be done by now and I'd have made it home."

He can't help the flatulence. So much wear and tear on his gut. He has nine feet less of intestine than a normal person after all the operations.

It can happen anytime, wherever he is. He eases himself in every room of the house, unfastening his belt buckle a notch or two, lowering the zipper, loosening his stance. He goes on talking, unashamed before his audience as if we might share somehow his primitive comfort in his own creature smells. There's a sour trace left behind him in the halls and on the stairs—no corner he may not claim.

"I didn't even have time to stop at the office and check the mail or leave my prescriptions at the drugstore, the way you've had me running around."

"I told the salesgirl you were waiting for us, I went as fast as I could. I didn't even stop to look at slips for the girls, their old ones are so torn and yellow from the laundry now, I knew you had the motor running."

"Since when did you care about keeping me waiting? Now I have to rush home just to make it to the bathroom."

"You poor man. If I'd known what agony it cost you to take me shopping, I'd never have asked. The girls have more than enough clothes in their closets."

"Shut up. You don't care about the pain in my gut or the pain in my head or the pain in my neck, which is what you are. So just shut up. I'm warning you."

Shut up. Glassed in. The windows foggy from our breath, that and the close atmosphere of the South that won't let anything pass. Dark kudzu overruns the ground, crawls over everything like something growing out of the mouths of the dead. Telephone poles, shacks, abandoned cars disappear beneath it until things are recognizable only by their shapes.

"Your daughter says she wants to be a poet but she can't tell holly from boxwood, she wouldn't know a redbud from a cherry tree."

Rain pours down the drainpipes and over the eaves of the houses. It goes *lister-pat, lister-pat*—he wrote it in a poem—flattening the leaves. Flattering the spatulate leaves.

"A father who's trained to communicate with young people, a poet himself, an educator, but does she take advantage of that? Does she pay attention, learn something for a change? I've spent fifty-seven years on this planet and she's barely had sixteen, but what use does she have for experience? Sixteen years mostly filled with tripe."

There's standing water in the sump pumps in the backyards of the shallow lots, the ditches are red running sores—things backed up in their passages like the chemistry of adolescence. Too many years of listening, too little chance to act.

"Just because you're an adolescent doesn't mean you have to behave like one."

Choke and throttle. Fumes, fuming. The car is the family's allotment of air, to be passed back and forth—him, her, him, him.

"How many times do I have to say it, observation and common sense. Observation and common sense."

"Women have no grasp of the mechanical universe."

"You don't see what's right there in front of your face."

And it's true. We know it. We can't see. There's always this film between the family and the world, this translucent envelope like a surgical glove, protecting us from the raw oxygen flowing outside. No escape, our lives will stall and backfire. There's only the endless car ride and the gray rain. The gray hair riding his collar, the dominant head. We'll always live first and last inside this capsule with its trapped smells of gasoline and bad breath. Argument, derision. Monoxide lifting off the asphalt. Methyl, ethyl, ether, wipeout.

Smell

I couldn't sleep. The insects were trying all the windows. I got up to go to the bathroom. I went down the hall. I stepped over the places where the floorboards creaked under the carpeting. I felt my way along the wall. The light was out behind their bedroom door ahead of me. I turned to go down the stairs.

I lifted each foot and set it down, balancing myself with one hand on the wall. I felt over the black death mask of Goethe. I stopped on the bottom stair. There was the white moon and the gardenia on the dining room table. I smelled it clogging the air.

I turned left at the family room down the hall that led to his study. I wanted to use his bathroom so it wouldn't wake them upstairs. I felt along the books in the bookcase against the left wall. The fingers of my right hand grazed the dust on the bottom of the portrait of Lee on Traveller. I stopped at the bathroom door.

I heard him in the study. He called to me.

He's doing something. In the dark. In his study. I can't tell what he's saying. I walk in on him.

He's sitting up in the middle of the cot, talking. From out of the shadows. He's in the middle of a sentence, and he goes on as if he was already talking to me before I came in. It's hard to tell what it's about. He's in the grip of something. I don't understand.

He tells me about a girl, his student. He talks about my mother. There are things he likes and some he only dreams of doing. "A bog, a nest, a ferny smell." He's written a poem in the night he wants to show me.

It's so dark though I can't go on, I can't see to. It's dark down in that study, maybe some birds woke in the night and cried outside his window. And in the hall I was afraid to go on, feeling my way, I don't know what I'll find, what comes next. There was no moon I think, just what came from the gardenia, pouring out the way a mother pours lotion from the bottle on her vanity table over her arms and shoulders, everywhere, rubbing it in.

Lister-pat

The sky was darkening. Thunder and lightning. I was talking to Patrick on the kitchen phone. I didn't hear the warning crunch of the tires on the gravel when the car turned into the driveway, I didn't hear the car doors slam. Even when Daddy thumped the kitchen door with the heel of his hand, once, twice, tugging it against the swollen frame, I went on talking and listening to Patrick.

The telephone was on the counter at the opposite end of the room, but he was there so quickly. He tore the receiver from my hand and smashed it down. The sky broke over us—he had to shout above the noise.

"Stupid girl! Don't you know you could be killed!"

Lightning! Electricity! What damn teenage conversation could be so important it was worth electrocution? How many times did he have to tell us? What would it take to get it past my thick skull?

I backed off from the blast.

Another flicker, a crack, and the storm broke for real.

I shouted, "You don't know what you're doing to us!"

His hand came down across my cheek, quick as a flash.

I ran upstairs and lay on my bed. It was raining at the double windows above the headboard and in the windows along the wall where my desk looked out and the skylight window over the closet. The whole sky was letting go, thick drops hitting the leaves, *lister-pat, lister-pat*. The room got dimmer as gray particles of dusk started filling in. Mother came in.

She came over to my bed and crouched beside it. Daddy was waiting in the family room. She said if I didn't go down and apologize, it was she who'd pay the price.

Remember everything he's done for the family. Think of the concerts and museums, the exposure to great literature. He took us through all the major cathedrals of Europe.

It was one thing after another. Things piling up. As if she had no idea. The rain coming down harder till the patter grew indistinguishable from what she was saying. The gray needles of light were thickening, everything full to overflowing, the roof gutters gushing.

And why did she have to kneel like that? It made the bed seem so much higher. A raft with its cargo, a daughter borne along above her mother's head. Storm tossed. Gripping the mattress.

I looked across at the wall where the man in the picture was so sick, vomiting books, pouring out his gratitude: *poetry, philosophy, religion, music, art!*

It's your fault, Daddy, you made me, you made me do it, you made me say it, if I'm a poet it's because you made me.

65

With your headaches and your hammering away at us, your sleeplessness—
it was insatiable—roaming the halls at night, writing poems on the backs of
envelopes and unopened bills, then reading them to us at breakfast, telling us
your dreams, until we were so full of your voice we could barely swallow.

And it's your fault I'm stupid, a poet's stupid, Daddy, you said we were
stupid and so we stayed that way, like waking up from an afternoon nap,
halfway in and halfway out of something, some part of the body that never
grows—atrophied, no, vestigial. Vespers plus virginal, Liturgical.

We had to box things together, Daddy, epoxy them, hammering and
hammering, pounding away at things, not always the right blocks into the
right shapes, too dumb to ask the first, stupid questions, and then too old—
Mother too—we had to pretend to know.

It's you, you taught me—

by the stealth of your footstep on the creaking stair, the slow cut of your tires
on the gravel driveway, the clash of the nightly arguments, by the racket, the
ruckus, the clamoring insects outside my window—

I smelled things out.

Boxwood, epoxy, oxygen, Daddy! Pencil! Paper! Write, write, write,
write, write . . .

I said I was sorry.

Sorry for what.

He stood with his back turned, hands clasped behind him, staring
out the sliding glass doors at the sundial on the patio.

Well?

The rain was streaking inches from his face.

Was there something about him that didn't meet with my
approval? Was he a failure to the family? Perhaps he needed
enlightenment on the error of his ways. A father should be told
when he's fallen out of favor with one of his daughters.

No, there wasn't anything, I didn't mean it, I didn't know what I
meant.

I looked around for something.

It was worth it anyway. It was all worth it, I said, for the poetry
and the music.

He spun on his heel to face me.

"Don't say that! Don't ever let me hear you say that!"

His face was dark as a thundercloud. As if he might lash out at me again.

The College Interview

It was two minutes after sunset, and the man at the liquor store said he wouldn't open up again for anyone, professor or garage mechanic, it was all the same to him, the law was the law, he was the one who had to live there in Mecklenburg County.

So Daddy had to give up his bourbon for one night.

He ordered champagne from room service and let me join him in a glass while we watched the evening news and then another with dinner in the motel restaurant.

The trip to look at colleges echoed other family tours. It had its educational value, even if I ended up taking the foreordained path and went to the University like Margaret.

I had an interview the next day with the Director of Admissions at Queens College, but that was still twelve hours away. Daddy would meet with the chairman of their fledgling German department—a woman no less—to offer his insights on curriculum development.

In Atlanta the night before, following his talk, the folks at Agnes Scott had put him up at the faculty club and me in a dormitory so I could get a real taste of student life, but Queens was too poor and tiny to offer accommodations so he phoned ahead to the Holiday Inn in downtown Charlotte.

He had me bring my notebook of poems to the interviews—even if I wouldn't show them to *him* anymore. He made sure I was allowed to sit in on a class—music, literature, or psychology, the triumvirate of my interests—at each school we visited. At Emory, across the tracks from Agnes Scott, the instructor in Beginning English Lit was nowhere near the caliber of Miss Love who taught the Advanced

Placement class at home. Miss Love cried over certain passages. When Nancy Sapp said *The Scarlet Letter* reminded her of a soap opera, Miss Love told us to pass our copies to the front and refused to teach for a week until we begged her.

Over medium-rare sirloins, I tried out some theories I was developing on books and music: I thought there might be connections between the different courses I was taking.

Daddy nodded from across the table, considering. He toyed with the rim of his wine glass.

Yes, it would be interesting to find out if Hemingway was familiar with Schoenberg's twelve-tone row when he wrote *The Sun Also Rises*.

You really have to read Gertrude Stein though if you're going to talk about Hemingway's early style; she was the true revolutionary.

He reached over to pour the last few drops in my glass.

I could start with Stein's essay "What Are Masterpieces and Why Are There So Few of Them," he said, he must have a copy somewhere in his study.

At home he never listened to Mother's theories—he always said ideas weren't her thing. I was the one he called down to his study after dinner to dictate his translations to—Heine, Hagelstange, Krolow. He said I was a great help to him.

My head was swimming. It was confusing. As if there had been an error somehow, a mix-up between the generations. Could time flow backward as well as forward, even upside down (retrograde) and upside down and backward (retrograde inversion) like melody in the twelve-tone system? Maybe it was I and not my mother who was meant to be my father's dinner partner through life. Had there ever been such a mistake?

The waitress interrupted to ask was the young lady through eating then brought dessert menus, and we finished the discussion of modernism over lime sherbet for Daddy and crème caramel for me—you loved it in Europe, he says, coaxing me to eat.

So much dizzy talk, and of course the champagne: back in the room we must have fallen right into our beds. The bedspreads were white chenille with a fringe like the one my mother used at home for the master bedroom—they were bleached till they dazzled. So white the color repeated, after I closed my eyes, behind the lids, the puzzling tails of floaters on my inner eyeball drifting up and out of the picture.

The next thing you know it was morning—a sky streaked gray, yellow, pink. We were side by side in the front seat of the car. I squinted through the windshield. The vinyl upholstery was sticky against my skin. Daddy pulled down the visor to shade the driver's seat, adjusted the rearview mirror, turned the key in the ignition. He sat back and let it idle—a matching sound rose through the rolled down windows from the insects in the grass and ragged weeds. He looked over.

Had anyone ever told me what a lovely smile I had, he asked.

I put a hand up to check my face. He put the car in reverse.

Pink
Yellow
Gray

Faint
strains

Clicks
Glints
Stalks

So early in the morning

A hair trigger
A straw grasp

69

Heart Like a Stone

The two of us on opposite sides of the card table, face to face, Mother's eyelids puffy, her cheeks greased with tears, her lower lip jutting.

Everything ruined.

It could have been a nice evening, she says, just the three of us, the other girls out for the evening, Clare with her party, Margaret on a date, we might have made a jolly time of it, things at least could have been pleasant.

All her careful planning.

She'd gotten me to take out the card table from the family room closet and open it up and set it in front of the television set. Together we looked through the entertainment section of the evening paper to find a program that might appeal to Daddy. It was a piece of luck finding that thing with the chimp.

And she hadn't minded, really, having to serve that way, bringing every course down the stairs from the main level, her back against the hand railing, sliding herself a little bit at a time so she wouldn't slop over the rim of the cups and into the saucers the way he hated.

All for nothing.

Doesn't she know by now, he said, how easy it is for him to spot her tricks? If she can't engage in normal dinner table conversation, if she isn't interested or even curious about what's on his mind, she should have the guts or whatever it is women have in place of balls to say so instead of putting this mindless garbage in front of him and expecting him to choke down his food with all of middle-class America guffawing in his ear.

He shoved his chair back, placed both hands on the unsteady surface, fingers outspread. Pushed himself off. He said we could look for him in his study if the house caught fire or something.

Water drips off her swollen features like rain from the flooded roof gutters. She blots with the napkin, raising red-rimmed eyes to me, presenting her woe. But I just sit there dry eyed, expressionless, not making a move or giving any sign. Fresh tears swamp her eyes at the sight of me, pitiless like that, hard as stone, not even acknowledging my own mother in her plight. Then something takes her body and wracks it, as if she's going to throw up grief, so she has to spit the words to get them out:

"You have no heart!"

Back Roads

I almost collided with the iron-haired French teacher on the stairs.

"*Qu'avez-vous, Mademoiselle?*"

I didn't understand.

"What's the matter?"

The school day was over, the last bus had pulled out from the parking lot, teachers were erasing their blackboards and gathering books and sweaters. The corridors echoed.

"Nothing."

I took my things from the window ledge and followed her down.

At the ground level we parted—"*À demain!*"—and I continued on to the basement.

It was a maze of narrowing corridors with the lunchroom at this end and the gym at the other. Heating pipes ran along the ceiling. I dumped my stuff in the stairwell.

There was a heavy metal door with a window in the top half, a wire mesh set inside the glass. It looked out over the parking lot where the pretty World Literature teacher, Mrs. Williams, was loading things into the back of her blue VW, books and papers. I watched. Hers was the last car left.

In back of her was a view of the athletic field, a thin stand of pines lining the farthest end. Beyond that the highway. At recess Prissy and I talked about how easy it would be to cut across the field and keep walking.

Mrs. Williams tugged the back seat into proper position. She bent to her purse, which was sitting on the concrete, to fish for something—I couldn't tell what. Then she straightened and turned and started walking back toward the building.

I dropped from my handhold at the wire-crossed window and faced the stairs. There was time to grab my stuff and run, but instead I went and crouched underneath the stairwell, hiding in plain sight. I covered my eyes.

The door pushed open and came back sighing, sliding shut on the vacuum tube. Then a beat in the silence.

What was it? What was wrong?

I must have made a sorry sight at the end of the day—blouse wrinkled and half untucked, hair frizzing, tears and pimples. The halls rang hollow. It was past time for everything. The teacher had a husband to get home to, everyone had someone waiting. The carefully made-up schedule of the school day was over.

Mrs. Williams took me to the principal's office. She wouldn't leave until she knew someone was coming for me. She wanted to make sure I'd calmed down since the scene under the stairwell, where I'd rocked on my haunches, blubbering through the grille of my fingers, "I don't want to go home!"

A wind knocked metal against metal on the empty flagpole in front of the school, where Daddy told me to wait when I called him.

It snowed overnight and on into the morning so there was no school Friday. Snow was so rare in North Carolina that Clare and I always felt we had to stay out in it as much as possible. We played like little kids in the driveway and tried to guard our front lawn against intruders but one of the neighbor's dogs tracked across it and then the mailman, coming in sleet or snow. Mother said it was good to go inside every hour or so and run cold water over our stiff fingers at the kitchen sink. Not hot. It was the only way to prevent frostbite, she said. In hot weather it was cold water over the wrists for feeling faint.

One of my future debutante escorts, Al, whom Mother liked for his good manners, came to visit that afternoon. He'd hitchhiked from Chapel Hill, where he was a freshman at the state university.

Afterward, I said I'd walk with him to the end of Darby, where he could catch a ride to the highway. I took from my purse the lunch money I'd been saving up—almost twenty dollars.

Three of four cars crept past. Al stuck out his thumb but they kept on going at less than thirty miles per hour, the drivers peering over their steering wheels, afraid they'd spin out maybe if they tried to brake on the slick roadway. Al was reminding me that the last of my excuses about getting married would expire on Monday when I turned eighteen, the legal age of consent. He said we could hitchhike to the state line and get married in Dillon, South Carolina, at the marriage chapel near the South of the Border theme park. A truck with massive snow tires and a Connecticut license plate pulled over. Al kissed me good-bye and climbed up beside the driver.

I turned back the way we'd come, but where the road forked, I went left and cut across the Church parking lot. The snowplow had been there—there were piled clouds of snow at the corners. But a new layer was already falling, whiting out the pavement again. One kid was still swinging on the playground swings.

I entered the tree line and the woods beyond. I could cut through it unseen then rejoin the road out of town just beyond where Al had caught his ride.

Twigs scraped my cheeks and tore at my fingers as I pushed aside the branches. I stumbled over roots. My right boot broke through an icy puddle and plunged in to the knee. By the time I broke cover at the highway just beyond the high school, both socks were soaked and my feet were starting to go numb.

There was no rush hour that evening. The highway was still only two lanes back then. It hadn't been widened yet for the overload of cars using the back way between the three towns, going to and from the three college campuses, the textile mills, and tobacco factories, past the old landscape of farm country.

I walked along the shoulder, which was steeply graded, keeping me mostly out of sight. It was a zombie walk the way I had to lift the stumpy blocks of my feet and set them down in front of me. The gray light was fading.

After a mile or so there was smoke from a chimney ahead and a lighted Esso sign. I turned in.

The store was an old shack, a wood stove inside, a woman behind the counter and a man on a stool talking, both with seamed, country faces. They nodded when I said I was visiting in the neighborhood and asked could I dry off by the stove for a minute.

I sat down on the rickety chair and took off my boots and socks and laid the socks over the grate. A radio played behind the conversation between the man and the lady—weather reports, road conditions. Nothing about a missing girl. But they must be starting to worry. No one in our family had ever done such a thing before.

My things were still damp when I put them back on. I started down the highway again, a prickling heat rising in my legs but in the toes—nothing.

Headlights caught me. A car pulled over. A man asked if I wanted a ride. If I got in with him it was possible I might come to real harm. I might never even reach my eighteenth birthday—the age of consent.

But I said no, I was almost there. So he drove on.

From our house in the Valley to the first lights of Chapel Hill was only six or seven miles, but with the rough going in this weather it was almost eleven o'clock before I saw them. There was a shopping center and then the bridge, then row after row of the numbered Quonset huts that served as graduate student housing. Their mailboxes clustered at the bottom of the driveway.

How many Williamses could there be? But then I remembered from the yearbook—Mrs. Robert P.

I could hear her laughing and talking with him inside. I slid to the wet ground beneath their lighted window, my back against the aluminum siding. Maybe I'd just stay there where no one could see me and listen to the sounds. But in a minute I got up and went to the door and knocked.

We talked in a general way about my being unhappy. Mrs. Williams thought I should see a professional. She mentioned the depth of my mourning for President Kennedy and the poems I

74

sometimes turned in for class assignments—in World Literature, English, even American History once. Teachers wrote things in the margins like, "See me after class about this." Or: "Your despair is chilling." I argued against her. I felt some questions went beyond psychiatry. You wouldn't take Don Quixote or Hamlet to see a psychiatrist, would you? Mr. Williams phoned my parents to say they'd bring me back as soon as possible taking into consideration road conditions. He was in his second year of medical school, thinking of going into something like dermatology where he could choose his hours and the fees were high, he told me, making conversation. He stroked his handsome chin. He wanted his wife to quit teaching World Literature and have a baby. They had old-fashioned ideas about family.

The sheriff was sitting in the living room waiting with my parents. Clare came down from her room and stood on the stairs dissolved in tears. The hours of waiting, of not knowing. Her own sister missing, maybe dead. The neighborhood fathers and sons had been out combing the ditches with the police. There was even a picture on the late-night television news. When Clare cried her features crumbled under the seismic impact of her grief, making the enormity of what I'd done suddenly clear. How could I have forgotten her? Why didn't I warn her—the one person who'd done nothing to me, whose love for me ran as clear as water. My roommate, my secret sharer. Her face was so pale—she had the fairest skin. I'd just been putting one foot in front of the other, frozen, in step, heading toward some blind goal at the end of my journey, someone to take me in, forgetful of the one person entrusted to my care.

Prissy appeared from the kitchen.

Everyone sat in the upstairs parlor while the sheriff finished filling out his report. Mother couldn't say how relieved they were. It wasn't like one of her daughters to forget to tell them where she was going.

The sheriff left, and the Williamses stayed for a while to talk. Prissy and Clare and I went to the kitchen. We poured Cokes.

Prissy told how she was the one who had figured out everything. When my father called her a third time, she had said to look in my purse and and see if the lunch money was missing. So they knew then it probably wasn't murder or a kidnapping.

On Monday morning waiting for the bus, Patrick said, "You sure know how to hurt a guy." Even so when I passed him in the hall an hour later he was with Nancy, buxom where I was flat, walking her to class.

After World Literature class Mrs. Williams told me she was proud of me for coming to school the very first day despite any talk. It was the first time we'd spoken since she'd told me good-bye, gathering me into an embrace at the door of my parents' house. The important thing was to move ahead, she said, think about my future. Learn from the past but don't dwell on it.

Everyone had a theory.

After the Williamses left, on the night I ran away, Mother had sent me down to Daddy in the family room. It was just the two of us. He stirred the ashes from the synthetic log he'd lit earlier and sat back. The captain's chair creaked.

"Was it because of me?" he asked. "Because of what I've been doing?"

"No," I said, guilty at finally having found comfort in Mrs. Williams's arms.

But he stopped coming to my room in the mornings after that.

I had to agree to meet with Father Bill every Thursday after school in the parish hall study. We talked mostly about books. I got rather passionate over some ideas I had about *The Catcher in the Rye*, and he told me I had a fine mind. He wanted to know what was wrong, but I said I couldn't tell him. He said, "Can't tell or won't?"

Things died down eventually. A few months later another teacher, not Mrs. Williams but the one who'd chaperoned me on the long ago United Nations trip, asked what was bothering me so, and I told her "I think my father's in love with me." But I took it back right away when her eyes filled with tears. I said that wasn't it really; what really bothered me was the war.

Prissy was the one who never felt satisfied. She always tried to piece things together logically, not knowing when I was leaving out major clues like what my father was doing to me. She couldn't figure out why I hadn't tried harder to get away. I could have gone to the bus station and sneaked onboard a Trailways bus bound for New York and lived in the Village the way we'd always planned. I could have run away for real.

In Life

He sends someone after Mother to help.

She protests she can go it alone, but he overrules the little wave of dismissal she makes over her back as she ascends the stairs to the ground floor, the ice cubes chinking in her glass.

"Don't mind me.

"Please.

"A few things, someone has to check on.

"Don't interrupt your story.

"Before the water boils away completely, and everything's ruined.

"Just ignore me."

But he insists.

"Won't one of your girls, please?

"Does it ever occur to you?

"Just once maybe without being asked?

"Things around this house—by magic?"

He's still expounding from the captain's chair in his corner opposite the TV. The evening news is over, the screen's a dusty olive blank in the intermission between drinks and dinner, the family room and the dining room.

He sends one girl up and keeps the other down there with him—if two of us are home—to finish listening to his story. Or maybe it's a guest, one of the neighbors or a student he told after class to stop by for the cocktail hour who now begins to overstay his welcome.

By the time help arrives, Mother's already poured herself the secret, third drink. A blast of heat in her face when she opens the oven to prick the potatoes. She refills the pot for the frozen peas from the tap and sets it back on the stove to start boiling all over again. She turns on the burner under the pan of chops, keeping it low to allow for the extra time. She catches my eye.

The golden circle of bourbon riding high at the brink of her glass.

"I just thought I'd add an extra ice cube.

"I didn't really pour myself a full jigger that second time.

"Your father makes his almost a jigger-and-a-half, but I like to space things out more."

She leans against the refrigerator for support, downcast eyes on the drink in her hand, swirling the liquid in and around the glass.

She says, "Sometimes I just wish I'd catch something so I could find a way out of life."

An oily coat of bourbon slides up and down the sides. Bitters. Bitterness.

"I'm not so fond of this life. I've seen everything there is to see."

She can't help feeling sorry for the student though, trapped downstairs that way. He probably didn't expect, he didn't realize how professors can just go on and on. And his clothes—you couldn't help but notice could you—she was embarrassed for him, the home of one of his teachers, maybe no one ever told him, he wasn't brought up in an academic household, but then they dress that way deliberately now don't they, trying to imitate the lower classes.

It didn't bother her, really, the way Victor spoke to her in front of him. But the poor student, it must have made *him* uncomfortable, that's what she felt so bad about. He must have been embarrassed for her. She doesn't even notice these things herself anymore, the people in her office would be shocked, well, you can get used to anything in life.

But her eyes fill and her nose runs. Her mouth's loose and softened, all her features smeary, blurred out of their natural state as if beside themselves, her face displaced by this second face. She sags again against the white comfort of the refrigerator. She's giving in to the soft, sickening thing he's made of her by what he's said and done—a quivering jelly.

"I'm ready to go anytime. Life is long—you'll find out."

Liquor sloshes in the glass. She's seen it all.

But she heads back into it anyway, down the stairs. He's still going, waxing preprandial over the dregs of bourbon. Hugo von Hofmannsthal, Hölderlin, Flaubert and Emma; how his own grandmother predicted that one day men would walk on the surface of the moon, and to think. Remarkable. The scraggly young man at his elbow attends: he seems to take in every word, eager as a medieval apprentice, with Victor his Meistersinger, the silver eminence he's bound himself to. He looks up at Mother's entrance. They both do.

She hangs in the doorway. Daddy lifts his glass, boyish blue eyes shining. He doesn't get her signal. An eyebrow raised, the little cough to clear her throat. She has to come right out and say it—how late it seems to have gotten all of a sudden, it's a weeknight for everyone after all. Otherwise, she'd love for them just to go on and on, she's usually very European about the hour she serves. But the meal she's prepared, well, she's afraid it's terribly simple, she's worried she can't stretch what's there to accommodate the extra person.

"If only Victor had told me.

"Feel just terrible.

"I would have put another pork chop on my list."

She serves it up to him. He has no choice but to partake.

Now in the night he must mount the stairs and find her there in the bedroom, her reading lamp still burning, the book lying open on her stomach, glasses slipped down the petite bridge of her nose. Her jaw's slack, a snore flutters her lips.

He storms in, in baggy pajamas, in midsentence. He's so awake he's almost twitching. She snaps back—comes to attention, pulling herself up on the pillows, her head against the silk case that protects her hair. She adjusts the glasses back on her nose. She's prepared.

She's ready for what's coming, what she signed on for those hours ago, down in the family room.

"You always!

"Don't give me!

"Humiliate. Embarrass."

He paces the foot of her bed, parading his argument up and down the room, the slit in his loose pajama bottom opening and shutting with his stride like a second mouth but with nothing to express except that view of darkness terrible to daughters.

Girls

Night time. Scratch and bite time. Rough insects and the tapping branches.

Voices wake me. What time is it? Which year?

I crack the door of my bedroom, hesitate, then advance halfway down the hall where the stairs begin. I sit cross-legged on the carpet. Here at my station I can follow what goes on behind their shut door. Nothing gets past me, I can hear everything, I can see by it.

He's sunk in the padded rocker in the corner of the room, a few yards from the foot of the bed just off the far right bedpost from Mother's perspective. His misery rumbles from that recess like the wheels of a locomotive still distant in the night but steady, oncoming.

"Mmm, mmm, mmm," he goes. "Mmm, mmm." Then a slot.

"What did you say? What?"

He can't hear her answer. She's put the book down, but she won't talk plain so he can understand. It's her fault he has to get up. He has to leave his chair—forcing the pace, back and forth along the diameter of the queen-size, canopy bed, across the view of her lying feet.

It agitates him further. The rumble spikes and breaks up. A bark, a trailing snarl. "Ruh-rrr. Ruh-rrr."

"Ruined!

"You always."

The girls this, the girls that.

Then she finds her note too, a ground bass that must have been there all along, absorbed into the electric current humming in the walls. It's woolen, granular, as if her voice moved on the gravel in the driveway outside. It goes on, monodic as plainsong, it goes longer and longer. The tedium could overpower him. He's forced to fight at close range.

In her face.

"Never enough! Always something more! She's your daughter, you solve it."

If she takes her glasses off, there's still a pane there. She can look back at him without seeing. His words bounce off, goading his fury, as if at the wild sight of his own saliva hitting her invisible shield.

"You're marrying off one of them, why don't you leave the others alone!"

Then the filler—her drone, her static, a steady surf whose syllables I can't decode, though I know from its run and spread how broad the beach is.

She says whatever it is a mother says into the dark in the hours when her daughters' backs are turned to the wall. The trickle of woe opens out, pours from her throat a gritty tide—she's been ground down so. It could bury him. He's being sandbagged. He'll have to use his forked lightning.

"Ack-ack. Rat-a-tat." He fires in her face. "Wendy, Wendy!"

His voice strafes the hallway. Patter-patter, puck-puck, the shrapnel scatters. But it doesn't touch me, I'm alert, it can't.

"So she never has a date, you think I give a damn?"

He's reached the door—his curses flatten at it. Then the exasperated struggle with the knob against the swollen, uneven frame. I have to scramble and scurry back down to my room to take up the other position, behind my door. I can witness the rest through a crack of shadow and light, a fissure of noise.

Their door gives way. He's shouting.

"Maybe you're right, who cares? Act Shit, Scene Fuck! That's what I say to *you*, lady." He storms into the hall. One last shot.
"So what if she likes girls better than boys!"

Ruhrr, ruhrr,
Hmmm, hmmm, hmmm

Over &
over

Toiling
like a hydrofoil

Plough
Rough
Trough

Practicing
tactics

Signaling his distress.

College

I was a freshman on campus when Margaret was a senior, but we were eras apart. Two out of three of Margaret's suitemates had engagement rings on their fingers by the end of Christmas vacation, and Margaret joined the club spring semester. Meanwhile, my freshman class signed petitions to extend the curfew at the women's dorms till midnight, elected a girl president of the now coed student government the next year, staged a boycott of classes in '68, our junior year, and a month-long demonstration on the main quadrangle on behalf of Local 111, the mostly black University Medical Center maintenance workers, and were teargassed by state troopers in front of the occupied administration building two weeks before graduation. I only got a whiff of the gas, joining in at the last minute after stopping by my mother's office on campus to warn her I might do something just like this. The year before I'd compromised with my parents over the student demonstration by serving behind the scenes on the Food Committee, making the peanut butter and jelly sandwiches that runners carried out to the demonstrators camping on the quadrangle where every passing townsperson and Daddy's faculty peers could see them.

I was always making trouble. Only a few months after moving to campus I swallowed half a bottle of Sominex tablets, or rather I told the dorm mother I had. They couldn't find any signs of such a thing when I was examined at the infirmary, but legal and medical precautions made them keep me there overnight. I had to promise to go to the mental health clinic for a minimum of six sessions, though when I'd fulfilled the precise terms of the agreement and refused to go further, the smiling counselor said she'd have to note her professional objection on my folder.

Daddy was very upset. When I came home for the weekend, he turned the car around halfway to the chamber music concert and drove back to check on me. He stormed into the house, Mother trailing behind. He shouted from the bottom of the stairs. Could he never leave me alone again?

Clare was the last one left at home, her senior year of high school. She wrote me at my campus post office box about how Daddy kept coming into her bedroom while she was undressing, and the night after I read the letter, I got drunk on blackberry brandy with my roommate, and the next day under the lid of a hangover, I wrote my first good poem, called "Sister."

Too much was happening. Margaret got engaged, Prissy got pregnant and dropped out of her freshman year at Chapel Hill to marry the baby's father, someone in the Navy. Johnny Pickett was a thing of the past. I was one of three witnesses at the ceremony, a bunch of fresh-picked daisies shaking in my hand. There was a momentum I couldn't control—earth-shattering events piling up the way they do toward the end of adolescence like late afternoon thunderstorms. Graduations, weddings, funerals, assassinations. Rituals with the ominous feeling of consequences about them, held in May, June, August, when the air's heavy and you can smell the rain just before it comes like handfuls of grass and weeds yanked out of the ground.

The next year Clare left for East Carolina College, a three-hour drive in the direction of the coast. She phoned Daddy from her dorm when she had cramps—he prescribed Darvon and a cup of very hot tea. She had always had the worst periods in the family, staying in bed some mornings during high school, face paler than the pillow just like the time in Gibraltar when I went off on the buggy ride without her. Daddy would come home between his morning and afternoon classes to tend her.

Her first semester at East Carolina Clare had a hippie boyfriend, and when he went on to someone else she got involved with a boy who had a disease that left him in leg braces and on metal crutches. She brought him home and helped him down the stairs to the family room. When Mother offered advice, she sobbed, "But I really love him!" After the crippled boy there was a married sportscaster from local television, and then she reconnected with the hippie from before. The last time she saw him he was waving good-bye from the back of a battered van heading for California.

She cried over pollution and the war in Daddy's study. He didn't want her or any of us mixed up in events. The last thing he needed was a daughter coming home from college in a body bag. Thank God Margaret would be safely married soon.

Love, Andy

I had a feeling about that marriage, Mother says, I didn't say anything of course, I never would, Margaret came to me the night before, in my bedroom, I thought she wanted the traditional mother-daughter talk, you know, but she said she'd changed her mind, she wanted to call everything off, she didn't think she wanted to be married after all, you remember she'd gotten into graduate school but she had to turn them down, I think there was more though, I think her worries must have gone deeper than that, she may have wanted to tell me something, about Andy I mean, there were things we didn't know then, but I thought it was just the jitters, you've heard of the jitters, it happened to me with your father a few weeks before the ceremony, by that time we'd already sent out the invitations though.

Well, there are mysteries in every family, that's what family means, I never talked to Margaret about what happened with Andy, it was between them, I never asked about his farewell letter, why cause unnecessary pain, I think Daddy must have talked to her, down in his study, I didn't ask, he'd never break a confidence with one of you girls, he was always good about your privacy, Margaret would have said something to me if she'd wanted to, she didn't like to worry me, she's always tried to please us, especially Daddy, after Andy, when she called with the news about getting engaged again, about Drew, the first thing she said was he's a professor and he owns a house in Virginia right in the middle of Lee's old stomping grounds, she knew that would please your father, when I got on the phone she said, "He's exactly twelve years older than I am, Mother, just like you and Daddy."

She was so excited she was stuttering, you remember how much that irritated Daddy, he was the one she stuttered in front of most, he thought she did it to annoy him.

Patrick

Under the sweeping college trees, in the green evening that's just beginning to bring out the porch lights below the dormitory eaves, he paces. Elegant and handsome, dipped and flourished like a fountain pen in his dark tuxedo.

I watch him from my window on the second floor.

He looks up but can't see me through the leaf-choked sky. He looks down at his wrist. It's time. A quarter to time. He frowns.

I know that frown, that brow, the way the high bridge of the nose interrupts his face giving his eyes their faraway cast, the flattened place at the back of his ink dark hair.

He's come to take me to his senior prom.

I live twelve miles from home now, in a red-brick Georgian dormitory set on a green lawn with five others—each one a novel of girlhood. All intrigue and jabber in the corridors, comings and goings, friendship, betrayal, and the great drama of reconciliation. And everywhere the scent of preparations, the sigh of fabrics, as if someone had stored bolt after bolt of material—for dresses, bed-spreads, curtains—in these warehouses of femininity. There are older girls to confide in who advise and console, making soft nests of their rooms to sink down in at the end of the long day.

Clare tells me how back at the high school they mourn my absence— Clare and Patrick and his younger twin sisters who always rooted for my relationship with Patrick. Clare has a crush on the better-looking sister. But not on Patrick. They pass each other in the halls and speak of "her." *She* is not here. As if they've formed some sort of honor guard around my absence—I'm like a fallen leader, a Kennedy or Parnell. Patrick coming together with beautiful Clare in my memory.

But I know the truth. That mournful Patrick roams the corridors hand in hand with his real girlfriend, Nancy.

Nancy's the school's accompanist. She can play by sight anything you give her the sheet music for. She's at every assembly, every holiday program. The chorus teacher wouldn't be able to function without her. They wheel the black upright from the rehearsal room to the auditorium and back it against the foot of the stage, and Nancy sits on the bench with her fingers suspended over the proper chords until the curtain goes up. At the podium, with the humming chorus behind him, Patrick reads from a script I put together. "A stone, a leaf, a door."

All over the yearbook there were pictures of Nancy—Christmas, graduation, Spring Show. In the chorus photo, in the far left corner, she posed at the piano, hands above the keys, face lifted toward the camera as if waiting to take the downbeat from the photographer. The teacher sat in the bleachers with her students—Patrick and I in the last row, laughing with our heads thrown back like a team of spirited horses.

He sat with Nancy in the photo of his own class as well as the one for Students of the Month. And there was a big spread one Saturday on the high school page in the local paper featuring a somber Patrick with Nancy and another couple, and the caption: THEY'RE GLAD THEY DON'T VOTE.

It was on an afternoon at the beginning of my junior year, just after we got back from Europe, that Patrick's mother phoned me to say how much it meant to her that I meant so much to Patrick.

After we hung up, I danced in the foyer. I hadn't been sure about Patrick—sometimes he chose me and sometimes it was Nancy. Now I knew what was in his heart of hearts. I turned a somersault on the carpet and my heels toppled the gold crucifix positioned at the center of the polished hall table beside Daddy's leather prayer book. Clare came to the top of the stairs to see what the commotion was about.

The first time he took me to a dance, his mother drove—he wouldn't be old enough for his learner's permit until spring. The smoke from her cigarette drifted to the backseat, where the two of us sat out of sight of her rearview mirror, holding hands softly, experimentally.

Our cheeks grazed during the slow dances.

At the end of the evening, he walked me down the driveway and kissed me goodnight at the kitchen door.

Mother was watching from the side window. She opened the door, then the screen—holding it wide to let me pass inside.

She said, "Just watch out you don't go stealing some other girl's boyfriend."

Everything we read, we became. We had World Literature together—Don Quixote, Prufrock, Hamlet. Words grew rampant as the kudzu in the Southern forest. I saw the reflection in Patrick's green eyes.

Faulkner wrote the forest, Thomas Wolfe hacked his way there, and at night Dylan Thomas sang in its chains.

I could hear it, trying to fall asleep. *Rikk-tikki-tik. Patrick.* The insects made a wall of sound.

He said, "Don't you think we'll get married someday?" We were discussing relationships down in the family room after school. Patrick wore madras shorts, loafers, and no socks. His tall knees next to mine had trouble finding room between the davenport and the coffee table.

Daisy and Gatsby. Eustacia and Wildeve.

I pointed out: "You don't marry the first person you fall in love with."

Having said it aloud, I could confide in Prissy. I'd fallen in love. It didn't seem possible that what happens to everyone was happening to me too. Under the false magic of streaming crepe paper and colored bulbs at a high school dance, reality had finally found me.

Prissy hadn't even guessed. She sized me up and said, "I never knew there was a body below that waist."

The heavy stuffed chairs with arms that curled into lions' paws, the marble coffee table in front of the velvet loveseat, matching mahogany bookcases on either side—glass doors, ornate keys inside their locks, the chiming porcelain clock that sat on top of one of them with the key in its face, which Daddy had sole charge of winding. Inside, the leather smells of the complete sets of Dickens, Thackery, Stendhal ripened.

Mother had had the loveseat reupholstered, this time in a sea green, when we moved to Darby Road. It was the same one that sat in the living room in our house in Marshall so long ago when she used to dress the three of us in matching outfits and prop us there—she gave each of us a Nickel Nip, a tiny wax bottle with a sweet, colored liquid inside, to keep us quiet till Daddy finished his nap. For years there was a stain on the red velvet to remind us of the time someone spilled hers.

Now I wore cotton underarm pads that Mother gave me fastened inside my blouse so I wouldn't get perspiration stains on the fabric. Sometimes even my palms and the soles of my feet were slick with sweat.

Not touching each other at any point, Patrick and I sat side by side on the green velvet. Polite with my father.

At last he adjourned to his blue books down in the study, but not before offering to write Patrick a recommendation to Princeton when the time came in two years.

After Patrick left, Daddy climbed the stairs to find me in my room.

He said, "This one's different, isn't he?"

Patrick sang baritone in a band with two other boys—one on guitar, one the banjo.

"Alberta, let your hair hang down."

His hands stuffed deep in his pockets, swaying a little, dragging the tune across the backup strings.

I watched with the chorus teacher, who was auditioning people for the talent show.

"Let it hang right down till it touches the ground."

His voice went low. Tonic, dominant, subdominant. 1, 5, 4.

A wedge of dark hair fell across his eyes. His shirttail hung below his hips.

I caught the eye of the teacher watching him—there was something unexpected in her look. She probably wasn't more than twenty-five or twenty-six years old herself at the time.

*   *   *

When Patrick got his learner's permit, it was like something out of *Who's Afraid of Virginia Woolf?* An adult must accompany you at all times. Conscious or unconscious.

He had to drive to the Emergency Room twice in one month with his mother slumped, groggy, beside him. The same sum on the odometer every time, a practice route: one half rescue, the other remorse.

Soberly he minded the road. Eyes straight. His outline riding in the driver's side window of his suicidal mother's green Renault—his jackknife profile that cut across my life.

The school bus picked us up at the end of our driveway, Clare and me and the other kids. The boys wore their shirts untucked. English Leather drowned out the morning clover.

Patrick came through the woods. There was a bee-stung look around his mouth and eyes from having just woken up. We stood facing each other, mostly not talking. He plowed a trough of dirt with the toe of his loafer. He chewed the inside of his cheek.

The World Literature teacher and the chorus teacher were one and the same. Mrs. Williams. I had her in the morning for one and then in the afternoon for the other. When I came into the chorus room I might find Patrick leaning over the piano laughing with Nancy. I wrote a poem about it called "Rebuff."

When I ran away, Patrick was out there with everyone else, combing the woods and ditches with a flashlight. The next day in school I passed him a note: "I love you." He hadn't been sure, he said. Even if it didn't always look that way, he felt the same.

After my picture appeared on the news, Mother was afraid I wouldn't get an invitation from the Debutante Committee to come out the next winter despite the fact that I was a legacy from Margaret. It might ruin Clare's chances for the following year as well.

But the letter came.

I asked Rusty, who played banjo in Patrick's band, and Al, both of them redheads, to be my escorts for the ball. Mother thought it was charming. Daddy called them "the two bookends." We had Debutante practice on some weekends even over the summer, then a full dress rehearsal scheduled for the Thanksgiving break, when everyone came home from the first trimester of college. It was two nights past Christmas when the fathers finally marched down the red carpet to give their daughters away and then claim the first dance.

That summer Rusty brought over a hummingbird he'd captured in his yard but when I saw the beating cage, I screamed, "Let it out! Let it out!" without a word of thanks.

His father had a heart attack in July when he rose in the orchestra pit at University Auditorium for a trumpet solo. I came home from music camp for the funeral. Rusty confided he planned to run away to New York but promised to come back for rehearsals.

Patrick was in Winston-Salem in Governor's School—one of three teenagers countywide who'd gotten into the elite summer program. Clare heard a rumor that Patrick had met someone there whose name, unbelievably, was also Nancy, but all he wrote on the postcard he sent me at music camp was: "If you only knew how I'm bursting inside."

In August he came home to drive his mother and sisters to North Myrtle Beach, where they rented a campsite and lived in a gay caravan like gypsies compared to my own family ten miles away in the cottage my father was still struggling to pay for.

Fine, stay home then, Daddy said, guard the family jewels, he'll go see the movie alone if everyone else backs out, he'll take Clare, it was something he thought of for us to do as a family while we're on vacation that's all, why is he sacrificing half his paycheck if he can't relax once we're down here, God knows *she* never cooperates, spending all afternoon cleaning baseboards and now this, this isn't the Valley, can't she take a vacation from appearances too for a change, the girl's not an infant for Christ's sake, she should know how to behave, besides this isn't some bum she picked up on the beach, she likes this one, or is that what's worrisome, if a mother can't teach her daughters enough self-control to leave one of them alone with a boy for two hours let them wear chastity belts, he'll go out right now and buy one, he'll buy three, one for each girl, mail Margaret hers in the morning, don't bother writing down their sizes, he knows them.

The scene was like a movie in itself—the full moon overhead casting Patrick's profile across his cheek. Knight of the Woeful Countenance. A whole year of high school left for him to finish when I go off to live on campus in the fall. He'll probably take my father's recommendation and apply to Princeton in the spring, maybe Yale too. Go up north to school like Quentin at Harvard.

Then he'll kill himself.

I understood in principle.

We walked back Indian file on a narrow path of pine needles and soft white sand to save our bare feet from the gravel road. Then kissed goodnight where his car was parked along the shoulder in front of our cottage.

My foot was on the threshold of the living room when I turned. He was sprinting up the driveway—we must have remembered at the same time. He'd left his shoes on the porch while we went for our ocean walk.

At the screen door, we collided. Two bodies, crash and burn. Like a movie when we kissed, as if the only air we could get was inside each other's lungs.

This time was different.

He took a detour on the way back to my dormitory. The car was the same green Renault he used to ferry his mother back and forth. Our headlights rose on leaves the size of platters where he found the turnoff. The dirt road dwindled to a path.

He shut off the engine and loosened his black bow tie. The overlook was steep, dramatic for this part of North Carolina: the new airport signaling miles away where planes were leaving the ground for the night sky. He reached over.

Next thing I know I'm crouched under the dashboard, trying to make myself as small as possible to fit into the space. The dirty floor mat coming off on the white chiffon dress I got for his prom.

He doesn't understand. What's going on?

He rests his elbows on the steering wheel and shakes his head. "You look like a scared rabbit."

He called me one more time—the summer after my sophomore year at college, his freshman year at Princeton—and asked if he could come over.

"I want to find out what's going on in that head of yours."

We took a walk from the old bus stop at the end of the driveway up to the church, then down the road in back of the woods behind my house and home again.

He looked at me and said, "You'd better go inside before you burst."

I swore I'd do anything he wanted to.

But he said, "I don't think of you that way."

He was right to say it. Prissy was right. I was in the dark. I didn't know what I meant when I offered myself to Patrick. I didn't know what I was choosing when I huddled under the dashboard. Everything below the waist was dark to me, the path disappearing into a territory as deep and mysterious as Conrad's jungle. Our whole house was in darkness, as if the sundial in the backyard cast a shadow that cut us off from the rest of the world, stranding us in another century, a European country. The rules were different from the ones our friends followed—we couldn't get our driver's licenses when we turned sixteen, our virginity was taken for granted. A different kind of time ruled there too, slower, stricter, classical, like the tempo in books—Dickens, Austen, Stendhal, those leather-bound volumes in the parlor bookcases. I knew less about sex not more, because of what happened behind those walls.

*   *   *

If I could go back, if I could find the porch with his sandals by the door, with that same moon, and draw him down to the cool cement floor mouth to mouth until he drained the last thought from my skull.

If I could find him as he came to me on that leafy college campus to take me to his prom and reach inside that night and separate the ticking chain of time from the noises of the crickets and the tree frogs and stop it.

Slippery

It was the driest summer in years, and when the first thunderstorm broke in August, I put on my bathing suit and went out in it.

My arms and legs were sticks, every rib showed in the gap between the top and bottom of my bikini.

I arched my throat and leaned back to drink from the sky. Then bent the other way, hair falling over my face, to let it run down my back. Rivulets traced my spine like the pebbly course of a stream.

It came down harder. It was the break everyone had been waiting for.

Arms extended, I began to turn, round and round. A dance in the rain.

Daddy was watching from behind the sliding glass doors of the family room, sealed in with the air-conditioning, in his slippers and smoking jacket. I saw him in frames through the blur of my revolutions.

I let go a leap. Half turn, half turn. My steps took the burnt grass of our backyard in slow waltz time. His beloved Empress Elizabeth must have danced like this in the marble hall at Schönbrunn. He keeps a picture postcard of her tucked in the breakfront over his desk.

My bathing suit was an unlikely green, and something in the nylon gave it a slick sheen like fish scales.

Later, when he got up in the night to write down his poem, Daddy said he couldn't find an envelope within reach that wasn't already scribbled over on the back. He had to use a church program.

He wrote about the swimming rain and a wood nymph dancing over the pine needle floor. A slip of a thing, disappearing behind slim trunks, eluding the knotted grasp of the willow oak. In the freshening downpour, the rooted oak dreams of spring, just one more spring.

Tongue In

He stopped me in the hall outside the family room at the bottom of the stairs. He came up to me and pressed against me so I was backed into the wall. He put his mouth on mine. Then he took my hand and placed it on his trousers, and I felt something stir beneath the cloth. He rubbed his lips around and flicked with his tongue.

I let him have it. I slipped my tongue inside and felt over the line of his teeth and the roof of his mouth, the base of his tongue.

I was home for the weekend, he had papers to grade—the others must have been out. Back at college, a boy my roommate fixed me up with asked me, "Where did you learn to kiss like that?"

Emma

He came into the lecture hall and dropped his papers and books on the desk, then spent a certain amount of time arranging them while he waited for the noise overhead to settle. He picked up the worn Penguin paperback with the lime border and went around to the front of the desk and leaned against it, propping one ankle on the opposite knee so it lifted the trouser leg to reveal a bright, cross-hatched wool sock.

He opened with the story of his Princeton roommate.

The fellow bursts through the door weeping, still in his pajamas. At twenty he's sacrificing everything to write his novel. He collapses onto the settee where Victor's doing his Cicero by the fire. It's over, he sobs. Only moments ago. His beloved heroine's dead—he has killed her.

The football player in the tier below me was laughing. People lounged comfortably over their desks and chairs. It was a story Daddy told many times at home for guests. Now that I'm finally taking a course from him, I don't really see much difference between what he says in the classroom and his dinner table conversation. His Comp Lit 101 is rated a highly entertaining gut course by the students who compile the underground academic guide Mother says has ruined some long and otherwise auspicious careers.

Another story from a few years later, at Stanford where he'd studied for the M.A. He and Mia had an apartment around the corner from campus, and he came home unexpectedly one morning to find their German maid collapsed in a chair in the front room. She was poring over a biography of Shelley. Daddy ran a finger over the dust on the mantle and asked, "How's the book?" The maid looked up. "Oh Herr Professor," she sobbed, "I think he dies in the end."

The laughter was general.

He took out one of the yellow slips of legal paper he'd stuck between the pages of his copy to mark the important passages and found his place in the last hours and minutes of Emma's life.

Every detail was a torture to her then: a heavy taste like black ink on her tongue, terrible thirst, then the sudden vomit on her handkerchief. "Take it out! Throw it away!" She turned her head aside when they brought Berthe to her—something the little girl said reminded her of life. Then she tried to grab the child's hand and kiss it, but Berthe shrank from her, crying out, "I'm frightened!"

It works like a musical motif. Remember? The scene in Emma's room, pages 128 and 129. She climbs the stairs to be alone with her unhappy thoughts—of her marriage, of Léon, of her disappointing visit with the old curé in his grease-spotted cassock at the church where, stunned with a revelation by the sound of the Angelus, she'd gone to renounce man and offer herself to God.

But Berthe was there in the room before her. She told her, "Leave me alone." The child clung to her knees and drooled on her silk apron. "Leave me alone!" She pushed her away with an elbow, and Berthe fell and cut her cheek on the chest of drawers.

There was blood. She was sorry for what she'd done. Charles came home and put a little plaster on the cut and said it was nothing, but Emma wouldn't go down to dinner with him, she stayed with Berthe and watched till she fell asleep, thinking what a good mother she was to worry so over a tiny cut.

In sleep the lower whites of Berthe's eyes showed. The bandage pulled her cheek crooked. "Strange, what an ugly child she is," Emma thought.

The last throes of Romanticism. The brute hand of realism at the swan's throat.

Remember—Heine died only a year before Flaubert's novel came out. His lyrics are so much more ironic than most translators realize. Writing and dying in exile. His "mattress grave."

How does the popular song have it? "The day the music died."

Someone hummed it.

A spatter of appreciative applause.

It was true though. Truer in the 1860s, after *Madame Bovary*, probably, than the gulf young people think is so great now in the 1960s between their own generation and their parents'.

A kind of trickster figure, Heine was, like the god Hermes, standing at the crossroads, belonging to both past and future, belonging nowhere. Jew, German, Parisian. "Romantic realist," Daddy had named him in his master's thesis. When he was a child, Heine cried and screamed so at the sight of an ugly playmate, the unfortunate little fellow had to be taken away.

Back to page 330.

Emma started vomiting blood, her skin broke out in spots. Monsieur Canivet found the thready pulse in her wrist.

It took a doctor's son to stand there at the bedside. To write the obituary of his age. The son who never forgot the stench of his father's surgery or the stifling alley in back where the corpses were carted away.

Everything choked him. Rouen. The stupidity. The petty middle class he was born to, reviled, returned to.

The body in that deathbed was his own—full of aspirations and vapors, petty misdemeanors, the failure to accept life, the longing to escape. He felt for his own heartbeat under Canivet's fingers.

The great Dr. Larivière arrived, but it was no use. He counseled Charles to be brave.

In the marketplace Monsieur Bournisien parted the crowds, bearing the holy oils.

In the classroom we bent to our books.

When the football player in the row ahead of me bowed his head, the bony vertebra rose in the soft nape of his neck.

Monsieur Bournisien rose to take the crucifix to Emma. She seized it with her mouth, kissing the body of Christ more passionately than she'd ever kissed a man.

Theme and variation. Echoes. Recapitulation. Flaubert said he heard the cadences pages ahead of himself, before he'd even set down the words.

My father read.

He blessed the eyes, the sensitive nostrils, the mouth that had groaned and lied and loved so, hands that reached, feet that strayed. His voice broke, recovered, moved on.

She's dying. The beautiful Emma. Dark eyes, black hair like his beloved Empress Elizabeth. The hourglass waist. The way he's described Mother when he first knew her in the Wisconsin classroom—she was so girlish in those days, so much fun.

Calmed by the Sacrament, Emma asks for a mirror and for a long time holds it in front of her, her eyes searching her face.

Was there ever such a woman? She asked so much of life, wanted to give so much in return.

How greatly the world failed her.

Remember the time she took the dog's long muzzle between her knees and stroked his head? Was there a more erotic moment anywhere in Western literature?

The one woman who could have understood my father, body and soul. Who would have been his equal.

(In the mirror a great tear rolled down her cheek.)

Or was *he* Emma?

Marriage

Mother was especially happy that Margaret's future mother-in-law was her sister in the local chapter of PEO, a sorority for women founded at the end of the previous century by four neighbors in the Midwest who vowed never to let their girlhood bond be sundered. Daddy was happy about Margaret's marriage because it meant she abandoned her plan to apply to the graduate program at the School of Social Work, University of Tennessee. He thought social worker a simpleminded profession, a waste of all her honors in English and Religion. He lectured her in the hot car out in the parking lot in back of her dorm: "No daughter of mine!"

They honeymooned in Colonial Williamsburg then came home to settle in a slightly seedy old neighborhood a few blocks from campus for Andy's senior year at the University. Margaret got the job of secretary for the Religion Department. The professors said they'd never been in such good hands.

Mother did what she could to help Margaret fix up such an old-timey house—it was quaint if you thought of it a certain way, she said. They had next to nothing. Andy bought an ancient upright for a hundred dollars and had it hauled in through the second-floor window. The keys were as yellowed as the nicotine stains on his nail-bitten fingers. He could play back anything he heard on the radio without a mistake. But he wouldn't play at Mother's parties though she begged him to.

She had such fond memories of how the three girls used to perform for company in the family room on violin, flute, and piano. Heady evenings. Professor Stroud of the Music Department who ran the Chamber Music Series would bring over the tired performers after a concert: Yehudi's sister Yalta, whom Victor tutored along with her brother and sister when he was a Stanford graduate student, or the New York Sextet—the three of us girls thought the name was a joke. Drinks, hors d'oeuvres, improvisations at the piano. The fiddle players feeling our bra straps through our slips and sheath dresses as they hugged us to their sweat-stained armpits—years later Mother said she wasn't fooled for a minute, she knew the kind of things that went on.

That first year Margaret was married, Daddy would pick me up from the dorm and bring me back to the house for drinks with Margaret and Andy and maybe one of the neighbors. Margaret and I used the upstairs bathroom together like old times—me applying lipstick at the mirror, Margaret on the toilet. A comfortable silence. Margaret had good posture on the toilet. Afterward she stood behind me checking her own image. Our eyes met. She was a married woman now and I was only a college sophomore.

"Just wait till you have sexual intercourse," she said mysteriously.

I wasn't even dating that much by then. Mother phoned me at the dorm in the middle of a Saturday night bull session.

She said, "Those other girls will go off and get boyfriends of their own."

She wanted to fix me up with Andy's brother Fred, the ROTC candidate—wouldn't it be cute to have two couples related through the same sorority? Andy frowned on the idea, though. He didn't talk to his brother or his parents, really.

His GRE scores were the highest in the history of the English Department. He applied to graduate school in Charlottesville and got a full scholarship, and he and Margaret found an apartment there in graduate student housing for the following fall. By spring they were separated. Margaret found a place of her own, a converted carriage house in the country several miles from town that Mother thought was adorable. The people at the University Press had convinced Margaret to stay on.

It was Daddy who called me at my dorm a year later to say Andy had shot himself while he and Margaret were on the phone. He was dead. Margaret drove over to his apartment complex and waited on the steps for EMS. Daddy said she didn't want anyone from the family to come up there or do anything—she was making all the arrangements. He'd heard from the priest at Margaret's parish who assured him she was okay, just talking a lot and chain-smoking.

He asked me, "Did you know she smoked?"

A Sick Man in the Hospital

Women never understand how sensitive the testicles are, he says, I told that nurse I had last night, you know the one I mean. Very black. Almost blue, she's so black. I needed her help with the bed pan. She just laughed when I complained. Can you believe it? She said, "Ma husband has two big ones."

You people don't know how they treat me here. No one does. You all think it's some big vacation.

Don't get your feelings hurt will you if I have to ask the two of you to leave a little early, I'll probably have visitors this afternoon, Luther's been wanting to discuss the department, it's not going to be easy taking over as chairman, I've tried to warn him, I've called Gerda several times about sorting through my mail and bringing over anything that looks important, and you can never tell when one of my students will drop by.

Don't jostle the bed like that, Lillian! If you're going to sit on it, sit the way I showed you. You're tipping it to one side, you're pulling me down. Off! Off! Go over there and sit in the chair.

Now everything's out of balance, someone's going to have to rearrange my pillows. Lillian, do you think you could bestir yourself a minute? Just stand beside the bed here and reach around me. Not that one, the one in front. In the front, the front! Right behind my head.

Honestly. You have some woman's touch, Lillian. Talk about a woman's touch.

I wrote a poem in the night. It's on the back of an envelope in the drawer. Later on one of you can find it and I'll read it aloud.

The nights are the worst time, the nurses never come around unless you're sleeping, you don't know what I go through, no you don't, Lillian, childbirth's a picnic, even a miscarriage, you haven't the faintest idea, some people are born with the ability to be empathic and others just aren't.

I know you can't call after eleven, don't you think I know that by now? I understand how a hospital's run. No, I wouldn't call *you*, why would I wake you just because I'm having a miserable night? I'm not that selfish. I'm not a monster.

You look tired.

The only one who was ever any good isn't here anymore. Nurse Wilson. Remember her? Yes you do. She was on this ward when I came in last summer. Older. With a twitch of some kind. Very nice. Polite. Interested. Skilled in a way none of them is anymore. She'd always ask if she was hurting me. You remember, I had that room two doors down. I tried to get it again this time, I saw it was empty when they brought me up from Emergency but they said they couldn't put me there. I don't know why. It's a much nicer room. A lot closer to the nurses' station too.

There's one very pretty young one this time, she comes on in the late afternoon. Miss Keyworth. Ellen or Lucy, I think. Very bright. I told her all about the origins of her name. English of course. Keeper of the keys. Probably one of her ancestors was warder of a castle, or maybe a prison. She was very interested. Fascinated really. No one in her family had ever said a thing.

She has an unfortunate voice though, it hurts my ears. I had to speak to her about it. She's not Southern at all.

I wonder what happened to my paper this morning. Not that I get a chance to read it when you're here, Lillian. There's a reason they call it visiting hours, you know, not library hours.

I think I'd like to be a little higher. Would you try cranking the bed up, Wendy? The crank. At the bottom of the bed. You're looking right at it.

Okay, now turn. Turn it. Not that way, the other way, it's going down instead of up. Turn it the other way. That's it. A little more. Now stop. I said stop! Go back. You'll have to turn it back the other way, it's too high now. Turn, turn, that's it. Stop. Just leave it. I said let it alone. Just see if you can find my buzzer so I can get someone in here to fix it properly.

The buzzer. It's somewhere under all this bedding. What? How can I find it when I'm stuck up in the air this way? Never mind. I said never mind. I don't need you rummaging around in there. It's no use anyway, they never answer.

You don't have to go yet, Lillian, you just got here, you're entitled to stretch your lunch hour once in a while after all these years, they know your husband's a sick man in the hospital. Wendy has a list of errands to do for me on campus, she won't be back till drink time. You want to leave me lying here alone again so soon?

No one comes to visit me, I haven't seen a soul from the department, only phone calls, and none of my doctors has done so much as to stick his head in the doorway since last evening. They say they want to watch me for a few days to make sure there's no more bleeding then they never come around.

Mike brought that joke book for me, did you see it? I think he left it on the window ledge, hospital limericks, very funny, you probably won't like it, Lillian, some of them are a little risqué.

This morning, after he finished rounds. Did I tell you Hans Hauptmann was here too yesterday? He had a consult somewhere on the ward, I told him my dream.

My throat's nearly dry from all this conversation. Would someone pour me a glass of water? The pitcher's right next to you, Lillian. That's it. My lips are cracking. I'll have to send one of the nurses down to the gift shop for Chap Stick.

Just lift the glass to my mouth. Bring the straw to my lips, that's it. Gently. Gently. Okay. That's enough. I said enough. Stop tilting! You're dribbling water all down the front of me!

Some nurse you make, Lillian. Just bring me a towel from over by the sink so I can mop myself.

I probably will have visitors now, just when I look like I've pissed the bed. Bad enough I have blood stains down the back of my pajamas. It's the damn calcium depletion, I have to scratch so hard my fingernails break the skin.

Maybe you can bring me fresh pajamas when your secretary brings you at six. You might as well have her drive you home first. You'll still get back here in time for the news. And don't forget the liquor store. There's not enough bourbon here for two drinks apiece. We need a new bottle.

Who's there? Who? Well, you'd better come in. This place is starting to look like a pigsty. I was wondering when someone would show up finally with a bucket and mop.

You women had better leave. They've probably been waiting out there for an hour while we sat here gabbing. You don't want to be too late getting back, Lillian, or they'll dock your pay. Then we'll be in a fine mess. Me stuck here helpless in a hospital bed needing every penny of insurance we've got. Call before you come tonight in case I think of something else I need.

Yes, they're leaving right now, I said come in.

Lillian? Darling? Stop. Can you stop a minute? Did you forget? Were you going to walk right out of here without giving your husband a good-bye kiss?

Bath Time

Bring him a different washcloth, this one's so old and frayed it can't do the job properly.

From the linen closet. In the hall. You pass by it every day.

That's better. He can't imagine why Lillian put out the other one with his towels in the first place, she never notices anything. Where was he?

Mens sana in corpore sano. Yes. *Soul on Ice.*

He soaps his genitals.

Why choose an incendiary book like that for bedtime reading? Look at those dark circles under your eyes, he says to me. Always running on your rims.

He tries to teach us moderation. He tries to set an example. *A sound mind in a sound body.* If he hadn't lived according to that himself, he wouldn't be here to tell us, the doctors have as much as said it. So many surgeries, the progressive dismantling of his gut and its effect on all the systems. His body demands more and more of his practiced attentions, it's become a kind of lifelong ministry. Roaming the halls after his bath, he pauses in someone's doorway, toweling himself while he gives an account of his dreams from the night before or maybe some further information about the Peloponnesian War. He has to stop sometimes right in the middle of what he's saying, reminded by the sight of his naked body to ask after it. Is that a new mole or only a pimple? There, over the shoulder where he can't see. *She* never notices, she'd never even think to ask.

Now that he's retired, and the three of us have our own lives, she seems to spend less time at home not more. The more infirm he becomes, the higher up she moves in her job. There's always somewhere else she needs to be, some conference, some convention or other, a grant proposal she has to write for one of her men. Isn't *he* her man? Isn't that what their vows meant?

He likes to have someone home to sit with him like this in the morning in the bathroom off his study while he bathes and shaves, it helps him get his thoughts in order. Important things come to him in the night. He barely slept last night his hemorrhoids were hurting so. He was worrying about me.

Nothing helps like a *sitzbad* with the special salts his pharmacist recommended. He was soaking like this once at three AM when he heard an eight-note hoot owl he couldn't identify. He told Frank he thought the bird said, "I've got to hoot, now you hoot too." Frank wrote back it was probably, "Oh my God, I've fucked the wrong owl."

In the daytime there's music on the stereo in the study—his records or the public radio station. The volume turned up so it reaches him in the bath. Schumann, Brahms, Mahler, Bartók, Poulenc. He rediscovers a composer and then for weeks submerges himself in that one voice.

The lush chords in the strings roll down the hallway and rise from the stairwell to find whichever one of us is home—a school vacation, a day off from a job, time taken away from a husband.

Clare comes on weekends, abandoning her own apartment—she's moved back to town after college and found a job at a clothing store where they pay minimum wage. She's on her feet all day, getting even thinner than I am. She's dating one of Daddy's doctors, a married man. I drive up from South Carolina on vacations from my first and last full-time academic position at Sandhills College after almost two years of wandering and temp work following college. Even Margaret, quickly remarried after Andy's suicide, makes the journey from wherever Drew has a job to tend to Daddy.

You linger in bed, the covers pulled over your eyes against the light, trying to postpone the day. Or down one flight, at the kitchen table—just one more cup of coffee. The obituaries. Even the sports page. But you can only put things off for so long. He calls. His voice lifted over the music—he has to come partway up the stairs, a towel clutched to his front so he can't be seen through the front hall window.

You descend through layers. The trailing notes of the orchestra, the steamy precincts. He wears a cologne called lilac vegetal. Pats himself down with baby powder. He has to be scrupulous—all the parts of him that have caused so much trouble over the years. In the swooning atmosphere of the morning, it's hard to tell his sickness from his health.

If you sit there on the toilet seat (he's put the lid down) everything he might need while he's in the tub is within your reach. It's good for when he's shaving in the mirror too—you're out of the line of his eyesight but available. Women don't realize what a precise, pre-

106

carious operation shaving is. If suddenly in the mirror he catches sight of someone behind him, his hand might slip and he could cut his throat. Lillian does that. On those rare mornings she's home and he calls her downstairs. He can't understand it—his instructions aren't so difficult to follow, are they? You'd have to *want* to thwart him really.

His focus on bathroom matters has always discouraged Mother. But what choice does he have? He's on the toilet so often he consulted his urologist about the gentlest, most effective technique for wiping. The man advised him not to worry over it so, he's never seen so clean a rectum. The pharmacist helps him find the softest brands of toilet paper, unscented of course. He doesn't want some cheap smell like a lady's perfume coming from his behind.

Soul on Ice. What did Malcolm X know about the care of the soul? All right, Eldridge Cleaver. Your whole generation chooses the wrong heroes, he says. If you don't preserve the body, there's no house for the soul.

He squeezes water from the washcloth over his lap.

You have a lot to learn about preservation in general, he continues, you have to tend the spirit, give it sanctuary, take care of yourself. Otherwise you'll live to regret it. Or not. The true revolutionaries have always had long lives, think of Einstein. Goethe.

The morning goes on so. There's always one more thing.

Why the texts of lesser poets like Wilhelm Müller best serve the lieder of Schubert and Brahms. How Schiller kept a rotten apple in his desk and every morning, before he could begin to write, opened the drawer to take a deep breath of the pungent decay.

What time is it? What century? Are we still in high school? Have we married? Grown old?

He takes the soap in hand to give himself one more thorough going over.

Hands Off

He told me right away what had happened, Mother says, he must have been pretty upset to confide in me, he dropped his suitcase at the bottom of the stairs and called me into the parlor.

Thanksgiving I think, I must have been at a conference or he never would have visited on his own, they'd just moved there, remember? Margaret and Drew, that nice condo with the sliding glass doors opening onto the Gulf.

She wasn't with them for long, the foster girl I mean, kind of plain, well *I* thought so, I only saw her once, they stopped by on their way to Drew's parents, you remember how he drove, Margaret had to persuade him we weren't that far off their route.

Well, you know your sister, she was trying to do a good deed, that was back when she worked as a counselor, remember, she didn't anticipate having problems, we have many fine foster homes in this state, most children have learned manners from somewhere by that age, what was she eleven? Twelve? Thirteen. Hard to tell when they're sullen like that, it's the teenage years, Victor used to say to you girls, "Pick your eyes up off the floor."

It was early in the morning, he didn't think anyone was up, he was going to use the bathroom, get his shave in and be out of the way, he went down to make tea.

He felt sorry for her, well, you can imagine, she seemed so forlorn sitting there on the kitchen stool he said, he wanted to make contact, we all need expressions of sympathy, isn't that what we're here for? Poor deprived thing, I guess no one had ever approached her the way say a father would.

She said, "Get your something hands off me!" Expletive deleted, I can't say the word, it's hard for me you know, such vocabulary, Daddy was shocked, when she shoved him he almost lost his balance.

No he didn't tell them, no, it would have upset Margaret, we didn't believe in interfering in a grown daughter's marriage, he was worried though, I'm sure that's why he came to me about it, having a child like that in their household, we both breathed a sigh of relief when she left, oh I don't know, somewhere, by that age you might as well just wait it out till you're eighteen.

Margaret's always been a good wife, but fate doesn't grant all our wishes, you don't meet the right person necessarily the first time or even the second, she was still in shock from the way that first marriage ended when she met Drew, it's the *families* who suffer in a suicide you know, at least I lived to see her with a nice husband finally, a house, and she's close to his kids too, that's important, you have to reach out beyond your life span, touch the next generation, well, you know, you've worked with children, people see how they respond to you.

Beach Bum

His students came back from the MLA in New York at Christmas in shock. One girl was found cowering in the elevator of the Statler Hilton at two A.M., weeping.

Graduate students, some of them with families to support. They'd work their fingers to the bone grading blue books, he says to me, for a position like the one you got at Sandhills practically just out of college. With time off for bumming around that is.

Now you're throwing it all away, just because you don't like the departmental politics and you say you can't write.

So the English chairman's an intellectual lightweight and a political opportunist. It's a two-bit, land grant South Carolina college, what did you expect?

Not everything is about the bombing of Cambodia.

You think there's going to be another academic job waiting in the wings when you change your mind?

If you can't concentrate on your writing maybe you're not a writer. A little faculty squabbling never interfered with *his* creative life.

Petty departmental infighting put clothes on your back and a roof over your head for eighteen plus years if you remember your childhood.

What do you plan to do instead, beachcomb for the rest of your life? Live off unemployment and food stamps in a seventy-five-dollar-a-month beach cottage with no insulation year round?

Your whole generation's like that. They think you can coast your way through life.

You have to eat to write.

Now it's this Poets in the Schools thing, don't try to explain it one more time, sounds like migrant work, what kind of living can you make that way, you think T. S. Eliot ever heard of Poets in the Schools?

Maybe you can move back to Winston-Salem and apply for your old position at Brown and Williamson collecting snuff coupons. Your replacement probably left when his Fulbright came through.

You don't have to observe every sorry aspect of existence in order to become a writer you know. You don't *have* to suffer.

There's nothing wrong with earning a decent wage. There's no crime in respectability.

Remember his lecture on Flaubert, or were you staring out the window that semester?

All life's a bourgeois phenomenon, a grotesque automatism that starts over every morning in your own shaving mirror.

"Will the Poet Please Come to the Office?"

Once I rented an upstairs apartment with a pink bedroom in a big white house in Roland, North Carolina, from a seventy-seven-year-old widow named Zenobia Howell. She was a large-boned lady in vigorous health with broad shoulders that were a little startling under her tissue-thin old lady dresses and scalloped white curls. She went to the hairdresser's every Thursday except for the time Dawn's mother died and Dawn called to cancel. Mrs. Howell sighed confidentially and said, "Why do these things always happen to *me*."

She kept her eggs in my refrigerator.

She left notes for me and mail on top of the bannister so I'd be sure to see them when I mounted the stairs in the afternoons after school was out.

"You owe me eleven cents in postage due."

She was one of the richest widows in Roland, a tiny town just north of the border with South Carolina. I taught in the elementary schools south of the line in Dillon, which was slightly bigger. A large neon Mexican in a sombrero welcomed highway travelers at the crossroads to South of the Border, a complex of fast-food restaurants, motels, and an amusement park, where most of my students' relatives worked. I knew it from the Fifties when it was just one restaurant and my own family stopped there for gas and food. It was the halfway point between home and Myrtle Beach. The area was flat and dusty, except where the Pee Dee and the Little Pee Dee Rivers wound through the countryside. Ropes of honeysuckle along the banks melted in the sun.

Mrs. Howell wouldn't let me cross her lawn with the honeysuckle I picked to put in jars in my apartment for fear it might take root and strangle her carefully tended roses. She made me go in through the kitchen.

When some of her dinner knives went missing she was forced to ask the old black man who mowed her vast property if he knew anything about it. She decided to let it go but told me in private, "You know they do love a knife."

There were three classes of people in the Roland: black people, Indians, and old white widows. A railroad track bisected the town, separating the big white houses of the widows from the other two groups. Even though white people claimed the Lumbees were a made-up tribe—blacks putting on airs—Indians actually ranked below black people at the very bottom of the economic scale. Teachers in the teachers' lounges told stories over lunch about the ignorant ways of their Indian students.

I listened from behind my copy of *War and Peace*, which I kept in a brown paper wrapper so I wouldn't be accused of being too smart.

I might have been playing at Being Somebody—completely cut off from anyone I knew, under the spell of my own thoughts, serving out some sort of imagined apprenticeship as a writer and penance for having grown up in the segregated South. I pored over James Agee's *Let Us Now Praise Famous Men* as if I were studying the grain in a wood table, read everything Eudora Welty had written, with time off for Germaine Greer's *The Female Eunuch* and Shulamith Firestone's *The Dialectic of Sex*. I wrote Clare advising her to take the temporary secretarial route and move out of town, sent subscriptions to the new *Ms. Magazine* to her and to Margaret.

But Clare had her own life, her own timetable apparently, leaving for Washington after Carter's election a few years later as secretary to his only female cabinet member, a former dean from the University she got a job with following the bleak clothing store experience. It's there she'll meet her future husband Richard, a civil servant. Meanwhile there was Mike, the doctor, her married boyfriend.

There wasn't anyone, married or unmarried, to date in Roland even if I'd wanted to, though Mrs. Howell had hopes of fixing me up with a longtime bachelor who worked at the local bank. She was the only person I knew to tell when I found out I'd won a poetry contest and my book of poems was going to be published.

"Why that's wonderful," she said. "Now you just have to get out there and sell, sell, sell!"

She kept tabs on the long-distance calls I made that night and every night and managed to work the subject into conversations she'd have with my father when he called to check on me, even though I paid her in full including my portion of the tax.

Like all first year teachers, I came down with every cold and bout of flu that swept the classroom. I sprained my ankle in the McDonald's parking lot. My father had suggestions for compresses and mustard plasters, but they would have been hard to find at the local drugstore. He recommended adding leeks to my diet, his grandmother always said leeks in the diet was a guarantee of good health.

My own diet was skimpy. I had a plan to save money so I could buy time to write: I'd never liked eating anyway and now there was no one around to object if I didn't.

It was an easy job being a Poet in the Schools because any idea you came up with counted as teaching but it was hard if you thought you should know what you were doing. I asked my students to describe what they dreamed at night. Some of them couldn't write at all. They made squiggles on a piece of paper and held it up to me and asked, "What does this say?"

I loved walking into a school. The dark smell of the over-varnished floors, the shiny corridors echoing with sounds from behind closed doors—gravelly intercom announcements, high-pitched chatter cut off by the single stroke of a command flat as the snap of a ruler. I wondered why everyone didn't want to work at such a place, the site of their original ruins, the center of the known world. Even the low-built brick school buildings from the Fifties and Sixties had relics— the same boring stretches of playground, the lunchroom smell. The old wooden desks scarred with initials that cut so deep it went back as far the Depression, when my mother went to school.

But Mother didn't understand any of it. What was I doing? Where was the future in this? Traveling from town to tiny town all over the state of South Carolina and then for another year across Virginia in a battered VW. Meeting no one. Both my parents addressed their letters to me with the title "Professor" though I'd only been on a college faculty once, for one year, before quitting, and I didn't have a Ph.D. or want one. My father spoke to the University placement office about vacancies at other colleges and kept me updated in his phone calls. He and I sent poems back and forth. Sometimes I drove home for weekend visits. When Mike could make an early getaway from rounds, Mother invited him and Clare to join us for drinks.

Even while he criticized me, I had the fantasy I was doing my father's bidding, although the life I was leading could hardly be set beside the example Rilke prescribed for Kappus in his "Letters to a Young Poet," which Daddy had given me when I turned twenty-one.

Once, as I was coming around the mountain, entering the hidden town of Bluefield, Virginia, in a snowstorm, my heart in my shoes for fear the clutch was going to fall out of the bottom of my car, I caught sight of the local high school and the sign where they ordinarily posted announcements for football games, dances, registration schedules. The letters spelled out my fame for all to see: "Welcome, Poet."

Bad Turn

How many times have I warned you about that corner, Clare?

You're lucky you didn't get yourself killed. And your sister. Killed or badly maimed.

Plowing into some Negro woman who probably shouldn't have been allowed on the road either.

What were you doing? Gabbing?

The two of you can't even make it to a funeral without some kind of disaster.

Shut up, Lillian. You're as helpless as your daughters.

When has any of them ever come to you in an emergency?

You don't want me to yell at her? Fine, I won't yell, I'll tell her how smart she is so she can go and get herself into some other mess.

The girl can't even read her own insurance policy for Chrissake. You want me to stand by while she bankrupts the family?

Of course it could. You think Clare's the one who ends up paying for this? How's she going to cover the woman's injuries on the salary of a file clerk?

That's what she's saying today but what about tomorrow after she's talked to her lawyer? You think he won't advise her to go after whatever she can get?

There's a little thing called pain and suffering.

Of course she has a lawyer, these people have lawyers just waiting for their calls, it's like a poor people's retainer.

I'll call John Hunter at his office first thing in the morning, I could call him at home tonight, he probably won't even charge me for the advice. He's a friend as well as a lawyer. He has women in his family, he must know about incompetence.

What was so important you had to take your eyes off the road?

How could you miss seeing a car that passed right in front of your eyes? What was the rush?

You didn't want to keep the corpse waiting in his coffin?

You have no judgment. Your spatial aptitude's underdeveloped. It's a well-known deficiency in women.

You think the phrase "woman driver" comes out of nowhere?

I was never in favor of letting you behind the wheel of a car, I was never in favor of any of you. If your mother hadn't failed parallel parking, she'd have been lying in a ditch beside the road decades ago.

Do I have to spend my days and nights waiting for a phone call?

Are you ever going to learn anything about anything?

None of you women can master the simplest task. How are you going to be able to run your own lives?

Shut up, Wendy.

Do you have something to say?

If you have something to say, speak up.

What?

What did you say?

What Did You Say

How dare you.

Who do you think you are?

How dare you enlighten me.

I'll say whatever I like in my own house.

If you think you're defending your sister by challenging me, you're mistaken.

Wait till she's in court. Let's see how they treat her in court. You think it matters how *I* speak to her?

Let her cry. You want to be standing over *her* coffin next time?

She's a child. You all are. You have jobs and apartments, all the trappings of adulthood, but you're infants. What do you want from me? She came to me for help.

You don't like the way I talk? I'm not liberated enough for you? I'm not a feminist?

Haven't I always taken care of the women in this house?

My *grandmother* was more of a feminist than you'll ever be.

You come home parroting back every bit of nonsense you've heard since you left for college. You think anything you say is original? I recognize every word before it's even out of your mouth.

Since when does having your period for twelve years qualify you to speak on behalf of womankind?

I've had periods. I've had your period and her period and her period. I've had Margaret's.

I've been through two wives, three daughters, and four generations of female students.

If I woke up tomorrow and God forbid God had changed me into a woman, I'd know exactly what to do.

Menarche, menopause, cramps, Kotex, tampons.

I know about women.

I know about women and I know about cars. They both leave a bloody mess behind them wherever they go.

You want to preach to me?

Who do you think you are?

Who are you to preach to me?

A former temporary secretary at a J. P. Stevens plant.

Do you have a life?

Toe to Toe

How did it happen?

Toe to toe.

My face inches from his.

Acting like a man, instead of a daughter.

He raises his hand.

Then I raise mine.

Clare stops crying. Mother holds her breath.

The vein in Daddy's temple pulses.

What next?

If he hits me, I swear I'll hit back, and then he's as good as dead—I'll send him flying.

He's an old man after all, just an old man. In his seventies now like my Creative Writing professor whose funeral at the chapel Clare was driving me to when we had the accident. We still made it in time for the closing eulogy.

For now I lie down in darkness and have my light in ashes.

Daddy sways. Off balance. Probably something to do with the hour—the fading daylight makes it harder to see, which aggravates the inner ear disorder that plagues him so. It's past time for Mother to switch on the lamps in the family room.

His arm falls to his side, uselessly.

"Bitches! Bitches!"

He stomps his bare foot like Rumplestiltskin. Turns on his heel. His face cruelly set. Then squeak squeak squeak across the room on the linoleum. Out the door, down the hall, off to his study.

Clare's sobbing. Now Mother. She begs me to apologize.

"Please! After all he's done for you."

"Tough shit! Tough shit!" is all I can get out. "Tough shit!"

Years later, after he's dead, she says, "I always marveled how you three learned not to express yourselves growing up."

Part 2

Life After Death

Silly Liesel

Every story happens somewhere. Dick, Jane, Sally, Father, Mother, Christopher Robin, Nan and Bert Bobbsey and the younger set of twins all lived at our house. I saw them. The spider climbed up our waterspout.

The chime that played "Hot Cross Buns" was over the door of the Marshall town bakery, and that was what the baker was humming while Father placed his order. He drove by the construction site near the playground at Oak Street Park and heard it buzzing from the saws the workmen worked across their boards. When he got to his office at the College, his secretary was typing out the tune on her typewriter keys. He had to listen to it from the windshield wipers when he drove back home through a driving rain.

It made him cross, it made him scold, it drove him mad. It started from a simple song his children sang, and then it got all over everything.

Sometimes we had to wear a sign: This Dog Bites. Something from Dickens. But we couldn't read it.

The Selfish Giant came on The Children's Hour *on the white plastic radio on the kitchen counter. It was five in the afternoon.*

The table was made, the bed was wound, the yard was set with snow.

It was winter in the Giant's garden. It was always winter. He was a mean man. Nothing would grow there. The children couldn't play, it was so cold. He disapproved of children. His brow was white with frost and frozen in a frown.

It was five o'clock. At six, the program changed to One Man's Family. *Some trouble in the low register of adult voices.*

He took us to an opera at the College. The boy was dressed like Peter Pan in green tights and a jersey, the girl wore a flowing gown. He knelt at her feet and sang, "Died for the love of a lady."

A child made the Giant's garden bloom. He was crying. He was too small to climb the tree. So the Old Man lifted him up and set him on the highest branch, and the tree and the whole garden blossomed as white as the snow had been.

His heart melted. He was sorry for what he'd done.

The other children crept in through a hole in the wall.

Once upon a time there was a girl called Bernadette who heard voices. She saw a woman in a mist. A fair lady. It must have been her mother, calling her. She's fallen down in the kitchen. Calling out. White as an icebox. She must have fainted or something.

A feint, a dodge, a gasp. A gap where she's been just a moment ago.

Fishy skin, still as pudding, stopped.

Time went on. The Giant got older. More gray. He watched at his window for the children to return, bringing Spring to his garden.

Refrigerator chunks, blocks of ice, ammonia spirits or maybe some kind of coolant, feet and knees turned to ice, a band around the heart.

It was still winter. All howl and rime.

He got his hat and coat and walked out the door.

There was one tree in flower. Grass and the Spring underneath. He ran over. He saw the child spiked in the topmost branch, all starred and furred. Pricked in the hands, stuck in the little feet. He saw the blood.

He cried out, "Who hath done this to thee?"

Upstairs in the nursery on Oak Street, Gregor Samsa woke one morning— which is after all the real beginning of the postmodern era in Father's Comp Lit class. Scuttle-claws tapped across the floorboards. His parents and his sisters were whispering behind the closed door out in the hallway.

Tap, tap, tap.

What to do.

I can still see the room quite clearly, with its one window, the light lying in a straight plane across the ledge, filmy curtain blowing, the optical floaters and motes wandering across his vision . . .

Seesaw

A bar of pink
a bar of yellow
a bar of gray

in the window
in the wall

A drone
in the zone
outside

the room of breathing

& moving

Tap, tap, tap
Who's that

He tries dragging himself after him—the legs are so pitifully thin compared to the rest of him. What's the use? This body's no good to him. Just a huge pair of feeler eyes. A throwaway shell.

Out in the backyard, Rikki-Tikki-Tavi chatters and trills his long war cry, "Rikk-tikk-tikki-tikki-tchk," and Nag slithers through the tall grass. He twines himself all the way around the hollyhock and stays there in the shape of the stem. At night he sleeps in an empty garden pot—he gets in through a little hole in the bottom.

The child smiled on the Giant. "Today you shall be with me in Paradise, which is my playground." And when the others came that afternoon, they found him dead, lying under the tree all covered with white blossoms.

There's nothing Silly Liesel can do about the hole. Henry tells her to stuff it with straw. If the straw's too long, cut it with a knife; if the knife's dull, sharpen it on a stone; if the stone's dry, make it wet. With what? With

what? Tell me, Darling. Darling Henry, my own. Water, bring me water.
In the pot, the pot! How many times do I have to say it?

But the pot has a little hole in it.

So Nag goes on living there, he can come in and go out whenever he pleases,
and the other things too, over and over, going in and out, the same song
starting up.

Mouth Words

Certain words she can't say. She hated it when he did. Put her hands
over her ears, shut her eyes. Hear no, see no.

"Jesus, Lillian. What's in a word? Do you know that expression?
Do you know where it comes from?"

In the middle of some of his stories, she'd have to leave the room.

"You're too refined to sit at the same table with me? Your ears are
too delicate for what comes out of my mouth?"

Four-letter words. Words for parts of the body. After he dies,
someone else has to fill in . . .

She says Gerda said it sitting in the living room right in front of her,
can you imagine, she was only quoting.

A professor, you know him, she tells me, he's known the family for
years, someone in another department let's just say he's in Languages
came up to Gerda at a party and said too bad about Victor, well at
least he's not suffering any longer that's good, a good thing for Lillian
too, she still has years ahead of her, she's always been so much
younger, she needs to get on with her life, it's about time she had a
stiff you-know-what in her.

"Ooo, I can't say it, it's not in me. *You* know the word." She nods
at me: *you* say it.

Some things she just can't bring herself to say, not every subject was
meant to be out in the open, she's always believed that, we all know

everything anyway, why go into the details, we all have bodies as it were, everyone has the same, shall we say, equipment.

And maybe she's right you know, why open every can of worms, what good does it do, some things I'm afraid to talk about, I think my sisters are too, certain subjects closed, even among ourselves, it's better that way, let the dead stay buried, once you say something out loud you can't put it back, I didn't want him to die but in the end I couldn't see any other way for life to go on—Clare pregnant then married to Richard, then pregnant again, Margaret marrying Jim, someone kind at last, finding work she likes, gardening, editing. I move to New York, first an apartment in the city then on Long Island, piecing together Poets in the Schools work and the occasional adjunct teaching position at any college in the radius of the city hiring starving artists. I like living alone, I can hear myself think. Whenever I can I drive my rickety VW down to Washington to see my nieces—golden-haired Marie, Charlotte who climbs me like a jungle gym and slides through my arms.

I visit my mother two or three times a year, call every Sunday, she has things to tell me, now that it's over, regrets, recriminations, tales from the past I've never heard before. I don't say much, I don't want to disturb her, if I step in she'll change her story, it's a form of power really, isn't it, listening.

Men pay court to her, widowers from church and campus. She's so busy with work and traveling for her job, it will be another decade before she has to retire. She won't marry again though—she says she doesn't want to end up nursing another old man to his death.

Well, you have to move on, Victor's a part of her past and he always will be, but she needs to make a life for herself, what choice does she have, it's a different world.

A new family, grandchildren who never met him, he's ghost, as the kids I teach say, part of his own stories now, time for him to take a back seat, find his place in line like a fading family portrait.

(Then why do I dream the walls of our house are bleeding?)

* * *

She says the word just isn't in her vocabulary, she must be different from other people, she can't understand meanness, it's almost like a physical offense.

She shuts her eyes, takes a deep breath and holds it, as if to ward off what's coming, waits for me to speak.

"That's it! That horrible word! I can barely stand to have you say it. Can you believe it? And Gerda had the nerve to repeat it to my face!"

Certain words she can't say so she puts them in my mouth—words on my tongue, tongue down my throat, my hand on the cloth of his trousers, her finger across my lips.

Child of Fortune

Some things go way back, way, way, way, way back, there's nothing you can do, we all have our crosses to bear, I guess that was his.

It happens in families, someone's always the favorite child, Frank didn't ask to be born first, he and Victor used to joke about Mama but really it was no joke, things never are, how she insisted on telling people she had two sons serving in the war effort when Victor was the only one in the army, she wore two red corsages instead of one when they took her out for Mother's Day, she said Frank being in the newspaper business was just as essential even though at that point he was only selling ads for the *Dispatch*.

Well, that was Mama, she was never on Victor's side, we laughed about how she wore black to our wedding but can you imagine? She said she was in mourning over Victor's divorce and being separated from her only grandson.

It's disgraceful really, choosing one child over another the way she did, I never could, you were your father's favorite of course, I guess it's true what they say about history repeating itself, he must have seen something in you he could identify with, you were the second born like him.

It caused a real rivalry between those boys I'm telling you, I actually had to separate them once during a fistfight, right here in our kitchen, it was usually about money, Frank resented Dad supporting Victor so he could get the Ph.D., not that Frank wanted one himself, when Mama bought the house in Yonkers for him and Harriet and the girls after Dad died he thought it was only fair but Victor resented it, we were so poor, just starting over at a new college, your father starting his second family.

Frank knew how Victor suffered under Mama though, he felt very bad about their childhood, there were things he told me in confidence, how he fell off the jetty on Block Island the summer he was twelve and broke his arm and Mama came running out screaming at Victor, "You've killed your brother! You've killed your brother!"

Things like that.

It's why Victor developed the relationship with his grandmother of course, she must have seen what was happening, people sense things, there are signs when a child feels left out, he spent the rest of his life looking for that closeness, he said it was a dichotomy, the Mother versus the Other Woman, it's in Jung.

No one ever could control Mama, even her high school classmates thought she was a terror, her parents were in despair before Dad came along, he got more than he bargained for poor man trying to keep her happy, he never complained, it was his idea to take the rooms at the Chadwick on a permanent basis, they all knew she was too high-strung to shoulder the responsibilities of running her own household, she got the best of both worlds when you think about it, room service *and* her mother's home cooking when they visited the boys.

Oh I know all the stories, the good times and the joking around, the funny things the servants said, but just because you're having fun doesn't mean it's a good thing, meals are an important time for a family but it's not enough, if God had meant us to let our mothers raise our children things would have been the other way around.

It was a privileged childhood I'll grant you that, nothing like mine of course, they had summers on the ocean, the intercontinental railroad trip they took all the way across the country to visit the San Francisco relatives, that was a real adventure for those boys so early in the century, but things aren't only what they seem, people don't necessarily remember the past the way it was, you have to look behind the words.

Dad did what he could, he was a saint really, building up the company all those years, he told the boys he'd provided for Mama so she'd never have to depend on her sons, of course after the heart attack it turned out to be a different story, Mama wouldn't hear a word against his memory but she said she had to let them know it wasn't quite the bright financial picture Dad had painted, she'd put herself in his hands her whole life, it never occurred to her to doubt him, she said she'd be all right if she didn't live too long, she had to think about what might happen to an old lady nobody wanted.

She almost destroyed Frank's marriage when she moved in with them, she thought she had every right, Harriet told me the whole story years later in confidence, how Mama criticized the way she was raising those girls and complained to Frank, she said the baby didn't like her, poor little Kate, she wasn't even walking yet, Mama would shut herself in her room and write to all the relatives about how badly she was being treated, Victor tried to intervene, he was very concerned for his brother, I don't know what I'd have done in Harriet's place, she made Frank choose, she was ready to take those girls and go to her sister's in Nevada, she had a sister she could go to, I was an only child.

I guess he didn't want the stigma of another failed marriage, those things follow you in life you know, people judge you, Clare says I should have left your father years ago but I couldn't do that, I had too much respect for the family, my mother taught me, she was just a simple soul what did she know about men, *Fly from him he follows, follow him he flies* she used to tell me, all this talk about divorce nowadays but it's not the big solution everyone thought it was, studies have shown, you have to think about the children, even a bad marriage is better than no marriage at all, Frank's other girls never got over being shipped back and forth like that between the two homes, Harriet treated them like her own daughters but it's not the same, look at how Thomas has drifted in life, he tried to stay in touch the way Daddy demanded, he wrote a letter every month after Mia moved them to California but she stopped the correspondence when Daddy kept complaining about spelling and grammar, Thomas was just learning to write.

Well, who knows if our own marriage would have lasted if Mama hadn't had the stroke when she was visiting us in Iowa, we were next, she wanted to move in with us, you don't remember, you were too little, we were so poor but we bought a new bed for Margaret's room and put Margaret in with you and Clare, that first morning when Victor asked Mama how she'd slept she said just don't put anyone you really care about in that room.

I did try with her in the beginning, I was so innocent back then I still believed people could have a change of heart, I knew Mama didn't approve of me, I was no one to her and you know what kind of family Mia came from before me, the San Francisco connections, Harriet said the family was determined one of the boys should marry Mia, I guess it should have been Frank, they were really more suited.

We drove all the way from Madison to St. Louis so Victor could plead his case, we thought we could win Mama over, he made me stay in the car, he thought it would be better if he went up alone, I sat there for four hours, I'd never do that today, I think.

Dad finally came down and took me for a walk, we went around and around the hotel in the dark, I'll never forget it, he tried to explain things to me, he thought I'd do all right if I could learn to flatter Mama a little, I had to call her Pussy Mama.

License

It's different now, you can fail almost a whole section and still come out with a passing grade, parallel parking isn't even a requirement anymore, that's what got her the last time remember? Thirty years ago when Victor let her take the test.

Yesterday was a big help, driving around the Church parking lot with me when it's all deserted like that on a weekday afternoon, getting in some practice with someone she knows beside her, Gerda's taken her out too, of course, after work a couple of times, and then the lessons, none of this would have been possible without the lessons, such a nice man that instructor, he lives somewhere north of town, one of those nice new sections everyone gets so lost in when they're driving her to things, he knows his business too, it can't be easy, taking out a bunch of elderly women and teenagers on the dangerous roads, he was so cute the other day the way he complimented her, he said he never has to warn her to proceed with caution.

Practicing is one thing though, with the lessons she knew there was someone there who could take over in an emergency, a man, this is different, it's the real thing, do you think she'll get through it with the officer literally sitting next to her the whole time, what if her hands shake when she tries to hold onto the wheel, what if she starts to feel funny, they say you can have a real heart attack from the fear of having one.

She should glance at the test booklet again just to check herself, even with all the hours we spent going over it after supper last night you never can tell, a good thing after all that the test place is so far out away from everything, it gives her time to collect her thoughts, this is helping, just saying it out loud, her fears, like she's sort of talking herself down as they say while there's still time.

Here's that thing about "going with a skid," she never really grasped it the first time, maybe she should wait another week, and this about the distances between cars, she has such trouble with the figures, facts and figures they just don't stay with her, she had that problem before, in school, it just wasn't her thing, facts, she's always done better with feelings.

No, you're right, she says, she should go ahead with it, her mother taught her no matter how bad something is you should think about how in an hour or a day, a week, whenever, it's going to be over, and everyone's gone to such trouble, even Gerda, you have to give her that, and the expense of the lessons, getting up early to have the extra hour before she went to the hospital, she never knew if Victor would still be there, well, she can't stay trapped in the house depending on other people to take her places, they don't seem to mind but she hates always having to ask.

She has to make her own life now, carve out a little independence, she only needs to get to the office and grocery store really, and Church, of course, that's her little route, she thinks she can manage it, none of the speed limits are over thirty-five, if she has to go out to the mall where a highway's involved her secretaries can drive her.

Speaking of speed limits, she says, you should watch yours, it's the unfamiliar highway way out here, well, she only wants to help, it looks different from where she's sitting, the needle thing on the gauge, a different perspective that's all, the passenger seat, the police are everywhere, hiding, you can't see them it's so deserted and confusing out here in the middle of nowhere, she's never understood why they put these places so far away from everything, no one lives way out near the Highway Patrol, and all the new people coming to get their licenses for the first time, they shouldn't expect them to be able to drive on these four-lane roads right away, or is this six, all the things you have to keep in your mind at the same time, merging on and off the on- and off-ramps, finding the right exit when it's really kind of hidden the way they have it—there! That's it, the turnoff coming up, you can see how hard to spot it is, coming over the hill this way, well, more like a rise maybe, you have to slow down now, gradually, so the other drivers know what you're doing, well, of course you're a good driver, all her girls are, she's proud of how we learned once we left home, but your hands aren't shaking are they, she says, it looked as though your hands were shaking on the wheel there for a moment back at the turn, you'd think it was me and not her going to take the test, my own mother about to face the test of a lifetime.

Looking for the Rainbow

I never really knew how unhappy Alec was until this trip, his wife was due in on the afternoon plane and he came to my room with some excuse about a mistake in the minutes, I was shocked when he cried, Alec never cries.

You could use a little makeup you know, you need color, some blush-on, otherwise you just look sick.

It's strange, I've always been on the other side before, I respect the family unit, you know that about me, and Alec is a family man, he has grown children to think of, and then her relatives, he's all tied up with relatives, he can't renege on those responsibilities, he's psychologically incapable of it, that's one of the things I admire about him, we just have to put it all behind us, it won't be easy but then when has my life been easy, he has to think of his career, even in this day and age they don't look at divorced men the same way.

No, I could never do that, that's his territory, my life is here, your father would want me to keep this house up, I owe him that much, for you girls' sake, and I could never be second to another woman anyway.

Do you want more sherry? I'm going to have another glass, it's so expensive, I saved it from the party, it can be your homecoming treat.

It's funny but I find myself drinking less now, maybe only one bourbon with the news instead of the two, Alec isn't a bourbon drinker but then he's not a slave to anything, he always wants to try something new, some of those nights in Hawaii after our meetings we just had rum and Coke and shared a salad for dinner, he's adventurous that way.

You can't get stuck in the old patterns, I never realized before how important that is, your father clung to the past in everything, pulling out the same notes, the same stories generation after generation of students, it's an advantage having new faces every year I suppose, I'm not criticizing, they all loved him, he was a different man outside his own home.

It's all right, I've got a handkerchief, I don't mind having a little cold now and then, it makes me feel human.

He never criticized me in front of people, that's a big difference, some women's husbands criticize them in front of people, I've never understood it, but then I can't understand meanness or anger, I guess there's something missing in me, before I met your father I didn't realize people raised their voices to one another, it just wasn't done in my family, it wasn't part of my experience, we associated things like that with the lower classes, immigrant homes, God knows your father's family wasn't lower class, those boys had servants the entire time they were growing up.

No one else ever spoke to me the way your father did, I never told anyone, the men I've worked for wouldn't have believed it, I learned to expect it though, underneath I'm a very strong person, I can take it, Alec knows that, he told me once, "People think because you're polite and Southern and you don't force your way into a situation that you're not tough, but you're no pushover."

He knows, we don't say anything, but he knows I haven't had an easy time of it.

The fact that I even got to Hawaii in my lifetime is a miracle, your father would never take me, he'd been there as a boy, all of them had, by ship, he said it was the only real way to get there, they visited all the islands, it was ruined after the War he said, only tourists went, he thought Europe was the important place to see.

Where was I?

It's different from ordinary relationships, it's kind of hard to explain, I've never known a mind like Alec's, his particular genius, it is a kind of genius I'm sure, he doesn't see it in himself, I have to encourage him, I try to be subtle, I don't want to hurt his feelings but he doesn't mind, he's grateful when I correct his pronunciation, he calls me his intellectual, I just help him put things into words though, that's what I've always been good at, I've never wanted to be more than that to any man, I've always been, what do you call it, you know French, a *femme inspiratrice*.

No no, not "who hopes," what's happened to your French,

inspiratrice, isn't that a word, that's what I've always been, a woman who inspires men.

They didn't appreciate Alec when he was here at the University, they were jealous and afraid, that's what it was, you know how professors are, all that conniving over promotion and tenure, they're out for what they can get, nowadays it's the Marxists, six-figure salaries and University Chairs, dressing like hippies in those sandals with their dirty toes, it was the Sixties that started it, your father was right, all those changes you people from the Sixties demanded, they could never produce someone like your father from the curriculum they've got today, or Frank, they had that classical education you never forget once it's yours, the term Ivy League really meant something when they went there, it was the best education Dad's money could buy.

But he never read anything new anymore you know, at the end, the last ten or twenty years, he said he'd already read the important books, he'd skim the first twenty pages of something then check the index to see if he was listed.

It's not healthy, you know what I mean? It's not a way to grow, a man of stature and reputation depending on the adulation of young students for his self-esteem, being told how wonderful you are year after year by people too ignorant to know anything else, some of those girls were younger than his own daughters! And the homosexuals, well, I tried to protect his reputation but he'd say I was jealous, I didn't appreciate him the way I had when I was his student and now I wanted to deny him the company of those who did, I was always polite though, I was never ungracious when he brought one of them home for drinks or dinner, I never let anything show even when there were whisperings all over the Department.

I knew, of course I knew, you think I didn't know? All that hush-hush business down in the study, the phone calls and the letters, it's not the betrayals, I was used to the betrayals, it's the secrecy, I hope you never have to find out, and then, of course, people said things to me, you know how people are, his Jungian therapist came to see me in Wisconsin right after we were married, even then he was chasing after his female students, she said it was part of his search for the Eternal Feminine.

Oh I don't console myself with that, maybe you do, maybe it helps you to think they were only flirtations, that nothing ever came of them, but imagine how it made me look, an old man running after his students, it doesn't matter what he did or didn't do, he made me look like a fool.

I won't do that to someone else, I won't put them in that position, even if Alec's wife is no one to me, it's she who's holding him back, people don't say it but that's what they're thinking, I've never seen a more disparate couple, she's let her hair go completely gray, they do look at the wives, you know, when they consider people for these positions.

Well, he's been through a lot, we don't talk about it but he knows I know, I just put my arm around him, that time in the room I mean, it's what I would have done for anyone, then he looked at me with those eyes and said, "Always remember, God gave us the rainbow," that was something when he said that, he never talks about God.

You didn't know? I didn't tell you about the rainbow? We saw the double rainbow over the mountains through the mist, it was just like the postcards, and Alec said, "You know what that means don't you? It means happiness."

I cried when he said that, I cried at everything we saw.

Another drop? I'm having another drop.

Not like those car trips with your father, remember? He was always at me when it rained, he kept shouting, "Watch out! There's going to be a rainbow! Look out the back window, do you see it, why can't you see anything?" Always yelling because I couldn't find the rainbow, those were the years I had so many stiff necks.

I told Gerda when she was over here, I had her the other night, I owed her, I said, "All the men I've loved are dead," of course she didn't understand what I meant, it's not the way it sounds, but she nodded, *ja, ja,* you know how she is.

It's true though, I have to accept this phase of my life, how does the song go, a time for this, a time for that, Alec and I both have obligations, I'm not going to start ignoring obligations at my stage, I've had my life, your father was my life, my problem is I don't feel old, the men I work with don't treat me that way, it must be something about how I carry myself, the way I move, how I sit, I just don't want to turn into one of those faculty widows with nothing to do but give luncheons.

Oh I know what you're saying, you're right, there are always problems in the world, people needing help but I've done my bit really, the panels I've chaired with Alec, world population growth and the rest, I guess I could write, like you, at least that's something you'll always have, that's unusual, you decided at a young age to sacrifice everything for your talent, you gave up the normal things most people want, that's your father's influence, everyone always said you're your father's daughter, the other girls knew it too, remember when your poetry book came out? Daddy was so proud of you, and so jealous.

Well, I'm not like that, my heart can't be divided up, I'm proud of all my daughters, really, I never dreamed I'd have three such accomplished daughters each in her own way, people still admire those photographs in the upstairs hall of the three of you, the three debutantes in your gowns, you all look so striking in those dresses, you could still look that way if you'd just believe me and try using a little lipstick, no matter what you become you'll always be Southern girls at heart, all three, you can thank your father for that, he gave us the South, he brought us all down here, it's something that shaped you girls' lives.

Begin again Finnegan
Whiskers on his chin again

Something to Read

You'd think he would have thought of her having to do this one day, she says, looking around the study, people never do though, they

136

leave their messes for someone else, well, it's something she has to get through that's all, we all have something in life, she can't keep living with the chaos though, bugs have been eating at that cardboard for years.

The man never threw away anything, he just tossed it all into boxes and stacked them in his closet, look, blue books, bills from five and ten years ago he never even opened mixed in with his personal correspondence, there's a letter from Thomas Mann somewhere, and the Schnitzler correspondence, he wrote to Hesse too, and he made carbons of all his own letters, she has to go through every box to see what needs to be kept, letters from all those girls and copies of his letters to them, the correspondence with that strange male student from Georgia who he thought was such a poet, musings written on the typewriter during his sleepless nights, it's a huge task, the library's been so patient with her and there's the tax deduction once the donation's made, scholars will want access one day, he wouldn't want some of these things to get mixed up with his *Nachlass*.

Words, words, words, everything all mixed up together, remember when he told us how he and Mia used to joke about teaching Thomas to talk using verbs for nouns, nouns for adjectives, like something out of *Casper Hauser* maybe, lucky they didn't do it.

It's good when there's family home to help, she was afraid she'd pull something in her back trying to get the rest of the boxes down from the closet shelf, Clare shouldn't lift anything either really, even at this early stage, the third pregnancy's much more tricky, you have to take it easy, well, other people can do the lifting, Richard and Jim, there's still room for you to sleep isn't there, she says, just shove the boxes out of the way so it's not so hard to get to the cot.

She hopes I don't mind sleeping down here when the house is full like this, who knows when we'll all be together again, it won't be long till Richard gets his first assignment now that he's passed the foreign service exam, she figured I'd actually prefer it, sleeping away from all the traffic upstairs, I'm the one who's always valued privacy so much after all, staying up till all hours reading while everyone else is asleep.

137

You did pack something nice to read for yourself, didn't you, she says.

Don't let it get so late you're too exhausted for the children tomorrow, you won't have many more times before they're living abroad, you're so good with them, your father always said every child needs an old maid aunt.

Sleepless

Words, words, words . . . I'm tired, Mother, I'm tired but I can't sleep. I scan the familiar titles on the study shelves, Jung, Hesse, Heine, Goethe, in English and in German, the English poets, here and there the surprise of a best-seller from the Fifties, *Marjorie Morningstar, Raintree County* where I found my first, secret references to what I thought was sex.

I'm tired, Mother, I wake up tired every morning, my bones aching, my body run over, hobbled by dreams, toiling like a guinea pig on a treadmill, tiresome, toilsome, the eyes glaze over with it—
Because it was hard, you were right, it wasn't easy growing up in such a family, it was hard just holding on, waiting it out, treading water, just trying to stay in place, keeping our heads above water, soemtimes I feel like I'm just holding on, Mother, trying to ride things out, storm tossed, seasick, gripping the edge of the mattress.

I take my pill container from the zippered compartment where I keep it safe from Marie's and Charlotte's fingers, safe from disapproving eyes. I look around at all the boxes at my feet, dig down into one and pull out a handful of papers, scan the top page without really seeing it. Words, words . . .

I write down everything, I think I've exhausted everything, if I get it all out, if I just tell everything, but the dreams keep coming, the talk goes on, Mother, your words, my words, his, unspooling from my head, my tongue, my fingers, coming off the landscape even, growing like kudzu, fattening on rusted farm machinery and abandoned cars, tobacco sheds, covering them over till you can only guess the names of things by their shape—Mother, what if I open my mouth someday and that's what comes out? What if suddenly I can only speak in metaphor?

I can't shake it, I can't get this stuff off me, if I could shake it from my fingertips, if I could break free, if I could see without this film over things, disenchant myself of dreams, if only I could see the world for just one day as it really is.

It's Dad's typing. On Dad's vintage typewriter. A carbon copy musty and flimsy from decades at the bottom of a box. Victor's handwriting at the top explaining how Dad was writing his memoirs for the children and grandchildren when he died. Almost forty pages, single-spaced, describing his adventures.

I settle in to read.

How he got started at fifteen when Uncle Julius gave him a job in the saddle shop. How he got into dry goods. His relations with the business and civic communities of St. Louis. His most triumphant deals. The characters he met along the way, those he helped out or tried to, the drunks and fools he finally had to abandon to their own folly.

Once he served on a jury with other businessmen and distinguished leaders. A case of minor fraud, *Smith vs. Bemelman*, in which the latter was accused of intentionally selling an inferior product. Dad stood alone, arguing for acquittal. He was eloquent. He maintained that the percentage of dishonest men was no greater among Jews than among Gentiles. Or Muslims or Hindi or even Negroes for that matter. He misquoted *The Merchant of Venice*. He ended with a flourish.

"Gentlemen, I myself am a Jew."

His confreres were surprised. Although they'd had business dealings with Dad for years, they hadn't known about his background or origins. Persuaded by his humanitarian argument, they voted for acquittal.

Dad made other conquests as well. For example, on a page of notes for future chapters that he never wrote there was the item: "Marriage Proposal: Grandma giving me hell until she found out I was Jewish."

Laundry

Oh maybe, she tells me when I get up the courage to broach the subject, a long, long time ago, she says, maybe they were, if you go way, way, way, way back.

I've waited for months, my Christmas visit, just the two of us so far, the others haven't arrived. We sit with our drinks, watching the evening news. My mother holds out her free hand. "Where did you get that?"

She takes the page from Dad's memoir from me and brings it close to her face then far away. Her lenses are smeared. It made my father so cross when he was alive she had to take the glasses off right then so he could clean them.

She drinks down the rest of the bourbon in her glass to the ice cubes in two sips. Time for a refill. She needs to check on things in the kitchen anyway, the water must be boiling, no it only takes one person, she'll be back in time for that story we've been waiting for, you know how long these commercials are.

But I follow her up. I think I'll have another one too, I say. Standing in the narrow space between the long wall and the counter. In the way.

She lifts the lids off pots and puts them back on. Opens the oven door and pricks the roast with the meat fork to see how the juices are running. She's folded the piece of paper I handed her and tucked it under the waistband of her skirt. It shows.

She measures another jigger for each of us and pours it into the glasses. Then the soda in hers.

It's funny, she says, but she finds she's not so interested in the nightly news these days, there's something in her bedroom she needs to look for, she'll take her drink with her.

So I follow her up the stairs, chatting.

Such a lovely watercolor she's hung in the spot where Goethe's death mask used to be, the lines kind of echo the silver stripe in the new wallpaper, was that on purpose?

The garland she's twined around the hand railing again this year does look like real holly, it brings the season indoors just as she said—more festive.

Remember how funny Daddy was about that? There was really only a dot of blood on his finger where he claimed he'd stabbed it on a plastic leaf.

In the bedroom she straightens the neat stack of magazines on the cedar chest. She adjusts things on her dresser and the things on her night table. Then she says she just remembered there's a package. A gift from the neighbors, she put it on the shelf of one of her clothes closets, probably the left, won't I get the footstool and reach up there, it belongs downstairs with others under the tree, yes bring it over, try the left closet first.

I talk to her over my shoulder, reaching up and rummaging.

I see her point about the artificial tree this year, I say, no more pine needles littering the floor and furniture, none of that constant vacuuming, and the miniature size being so much more convenient so you don't end up with Christmas all over the floor the way we used to.

But she doesn't hear me. She's gone. The sounds come from the adjoining bath—she's closed the door partway. It's going one step too far to follow her in while she pulls down her pants and uses the toilet.

The noise of the television rises through the floorboards, continuing down in the family room, where we've abandoned our most faithful family ritual.

Flushing toilet. The faucet—on, off. Time for a dab at the hand towel, and she comes out. Adjusting her skirt so the zipper's on the left, tugging it into place.

141

Nothing at the waistband. Not in her hands either. She takes her glass from the night table where she set it down and brushes past me.

It may not be too late. That commentator Victor used to admire so, what's-his-name, comes on at the very end doesn't he, we might just catch it, she says. Well, do it fast then, he always has something interesting to say.

Everything's in order in the bathroom when I go in. Back brush, bottle of lotion on the side of the tub. Bath beads in their plastic box. I open the medicine cabinet: Bufferin and Alka-Seltzer, mouthwash, a reel of floss next to a box of toothpicks. Neat, minimal. The store of someone who medicates cautiously, wary of introducing foreign substances into the body. On the shelves in the downstairs bathroom by his study, my father always had something for every kind of pain he felt.

I turn and lower the seat. Sit down. Stare. The toilet paper roll. The new green hamper. I open the lid and shut it. Open it again.

Crumpled into a ball and left right on top. No attempt to bury it under the dirty clothes and towels stuffed inside. I take it out and try to smooth the creases from the ancient typing.

A Few Simple Questions

Why do all these contemporary writers always have to write about their childhoods?

Why all these women writers?

This new generation, your generation, a generation younger than you.

One of these really great new young Southern writers I keep hearing about.

Those Irish writers always crying in their beers.

Why do they publish such things?

When are *you* going to publish something?

Why do writers always have to publish?

Why do writers always have to write?

These women in their twenties, thirties, forties
> women writers in their fifties
> you people from the Sixties
> professors, poets, homosexual Marxist professors, barefoot, sandals, with their dirty toes, I don't like to say Jewish but why do feminists, blacks, those Women's Studies people always have to?

Keeper

I could have called Margaret but she's got such a busy schedule these days, I didn't want to upset her whole week, then she feels she has to call me every day, and Clare with the new baby not to mention the time difference in Venezuela, you're better with this kind of thing anyway, you don't get upset, I hope the weather's not too bad up there near you.

Well, it's just that I had one of my spells, you know those spells I get when my heart starts beating and the hands get shaky, it's been quite a while, kind of a setback really.

Tuesday night. I'd just gotten back from my meeting at Church with the Outreach Committee, you knew I'm on Outreach didn't you, wait that was Monday, was it Monday or Tuesday, what day is it today? Well, anyway.

I'd spent the whole day in the study going through Daddy's boxes trying to organize things so I can get started on the taxes, I have to get everything ready to take to the man, you know the one I go to, my old friend, what's-his-name, oh no not that old man, the one in the wheelchair? That was years ago, he finally went to jail, I don't know why Victor insisted on going to him.

I'm in real trouble though, I told you didn't I, the government's saying I owe back taxes, it's from years ago, before Daddy died, I don't know how I'm going to come up with it, I'll have to cut back on something.

I thought it must be the coffee, I let the men pour me half a cup after the meeting, you know my Outreach men, they're all so sweet, they swore it was decaffeinated but I don't think that really makes any difference do you, I still get nervous afterward, you knew I'd stopped drinking coffee in the mornings, yes I've been having tea instead, can you believe it, after all those years with your father and his tea bags, he'd say I didn't steep it long enough or else I let it go too long and the tea got cold, well, I'm not fussy that way, I've even started liking the taste.

It's hard at the office, there's always coffee, the smell, my boss coming in to see me with his cup, I have a new boss you know, no, Plonsky, Dick Plonsky, Pritchard left, but I was telling you about the business with the coffee, this must be costing you a fortune.

My secretaries are always standing around the coffee machine on their breaks and it's important for me to socialize, people don't like to work for someone who's all business, I try bringing a tea bag with me in the mornings but I'm always so rushed, it's all I can do to pack my container of yogurt and a piece of fruit.

Well, I'd been up the night before till two or three reading my book maybe that was it, terrible book by the way, *Sassafras*-something I think it's called, I don't remember, I really want to get back to that wonderful new history of Poland but I can't seem to put this down even if it is trash, it's by that new young Southern writer, I'm sure you've heard of him, younger than you, a different generation, he's a huge success, I'm not saying he isn't talented but really, some of these things I simply don't want to know about, I don't see why I should have to, wife beating, divorce, copulation, and there's nothing particularly Southern about it, the way the characters talk they could just as easily be from some hick town out west, well, you know my theory, you don't? I have a theory about these novels they're writing now, I can tell *you*, you're my literary daughter, I think they don't know how to create real characters anymore, you know what I mean? They're not like the people in books used to be, not like Dickens or, you know, Thackeray, they're just not real, not like the people *I* know anyway, they're not the nice ladies who do the altar flowers at Church every week or the young man who helps me at my bank branch, why does no one ever write about *those* people, it's something to think about, I bet you could really start something with that, unsung heroes, you should bring it up with some of your writer friends up there.

Well, I guess I'll just come right out and tell you.

About the spell.

You remember what happens, the shaking and the flashing lights in my eyes, I haven't had it in so long I thought maybe I was over them, I could have called next door, Pete would have come right over, he doesn't mind being disturbed but I mind it, I know he has to get up early with the dogs so I finally called Gerda, she's awake till all hours talking on the phone with that friend of hers and anyway she owes me, and you know how much she loves being in on things.

She came to my rescue, I have to give her that, she was the one who remembered what day it was, I mean the date, and when I told her what I'd been doing she said "no wonder you're shaking, Lillian!"

All those hours down in the study surrounded by his things, it's such a dark depressing room anyway, for years I begged him to let me get new curtains but I can't even think about things like that until I've made some headway with the boxes, there never seems to be any end in sight, maybe if you came down here or Margaret when she's not so busy.

I can't keep living with the house looking this way, Gerda agreed, she understands my position or at least she pretends to, I have to remember always to take her with a grain of salt but she did know Daddy, and she understands about houses, you know she just moved into that big new expensive one.

You have to make your own territory, when your father was alive it was a different thing, I kept the house the way he wanted but those were never *my* interests, what does Franz Josef have to do with my life, I have my own interests in life, it's not just the redecorating though, this house needs major repairs, it's in terrible shape, oh yes, the cracks in the foundation, he got the man out here to look at them once but then he didn't like the estimate.

It's not good to let a house go for so long, it needs painting inside and out, I don't know how I'll manage it, I'm still paying for the sofa and chairs, that was a big expense after he died but everyone said it was important for me to do, that's not my real problem though, my real problem is whether to stay here at all, someone my age, I've been meaning to talk to you, I'd really like your opinion, after all you're my daughter who lives alone.

I keep asking myself what I'm supposed to do with all his things, keep them until I die and then let you girls worry about it? Of course I may go tomorrow but then again I could live another twenty years, people do you know.

Clare and Margaret have their lives, they have families, I could never be the interfering mother-in-law, I wonder if you've ever thought about relocating, I don't know how you can bear it in that dirty city, everyone wants to live down here now you know, it's not the South you grew up in, all your old friends are moving back, maybe once I get the house in shape you'll want to think about it.

You don't know what it's like for me, I finish one box and there are still a dozen more in the closet, old term papers, love letters, it's all I can do to make myself read them, what's-her-name the blonde, that went on for years, he practically dragged her through the M.A. program, spoon-feeding her his own ideas, it's all in the letters, all that Jungian anima animus talk he went on about, you remember, the search for his female opposite, I'm telling you that girl wasn't up to being anyone's anima, all she wanted was to meet some rich fellow.

Oh my feelings aren't hurt, my feelings can't be hurt, I swallowed my pride years ago, I'm embarrassed for *his* sake.

Everything he ever accomplished is down in that study, he wrote everything down, I keep finding his handwriting on the backs of envelopes, lists of his errands, notes for poems, lines, even at the bottom of some old hospital menu, the man was obsessed with words, it's sad really, he never gave up hope.

I don't know what to do with all of it, that's the problem, I can't live my life as the keeper of his flame.

Well, it's not for *you* to worry about, it's my business, something for me to hash over with myself in the dark hours of the night, the dark hour of the soul I think Daddy used to call it when he couldn't sleep, I just wanted to tell you about the nervousness.

You remember what happened the first year, you don't? Gerda reminded me, it all came back to me when we were talking on the phone.

I had that long weekend conference way out at the Center with my Planning Board, we're all so close, with my schedule the way it is I should resign but they beg me every year and I do love to see the flowers, you know the gorgeous planting they do at the Center, the daffodils are usually coming up about the time we have annual meeting.

Well, I was lucky, two of the leading heart specialists in the U.S. were there, some big medical thing the University was sponsoring, I had to laugh afterward the way they all rushed around for me, I told them there's not another place in the country where you can get this kind of service, all the really big names in medicine come here you know.

They were scrupulous with me, they took every precaution, checking my pulse and everything, then right in the middle of the exam I realized it was the same room.

The same room.

I guess I'd sort of come round by that time, I started taking in my surroundings and then all of a sudden I remembered they put your father and me in that same room the last time he came out there, you know, before he went in the hospital, remember how he liked to come along sometimes when I had meetings so he could use the pool, I couldn't believe it, the same bedroom, even the bed, I don't know why I didn't pick the other bed to sleep in.

As soon as I thought of it I started to feel better, the flashing lights went away, my heart stopped racing, I couldn't tell the medical people that, of course, they'd gone to so much trouble.

Whew, it's good to get the whole thing off my chest, you're a good listener, I'm glad you called, or I called you and you called back, I'm glad we went over all of it, that had to be what caused the spell on

147

Monday too I'm sure, Tuesday I mean, it must have been the memory
of your father.

> Every day the same
> day coming to the door
> the blue-lined notebook paper
> and the spiral binding
> the spiral binding
>
> long division on the horizon
> the banded iris dawning

Small Talk

Hadley almost fell out of her seat, she couldn't believe I'd never
suspected we were Jewish, she's been waiting twenty years for me to
ask.

Aunt Harriet says maybe Lillian was afraid, raising three girls
down there, three future debutantes.

We all stop talking to listen to the announcement.

Chicago . . . Flight delay. But it's some other airline.

When they were old enough to have it explained, Hadley
remembers, Frank told Hadley and Kate he'd made his brother a
promise not to tell us, but it was his promise not theirs, they were free
to make their own decision, he would never ask his daughters to lie.

Aunt Harriet says she always thought Victor stopped bringing the
family with him for visits because of it, not that they kept kosher or
anything remotely like that, maybe he was afraid even in a non-
observant household something might show.

The hardest time for her, Hadley says, was Margaret's first
wedding when she had to sit through that long Episcopal service
with everyone and keep her mouth shut. Her father had explained to
them their uncle's important position in the congregation.

Oh remember the 1957 visit when Kate announced to everyone that she was a Confucian? The other four of us girls interviewed her using Uncle Frank's pocket Dictaphone, and she answered every question with "Confucius say."

"Confucius say, 'Ask the ancestors.'"

"Confucius say, 'Better living with chemistry.'"

Hadley laughs until we have to pound her on the back—just like her father. Someone remember to tell Kate.

Aunt Harriet says the family always talks this much.

Then it's time.

We gather our coats and purses from the far end of the booth and walk together to the departure gate where Harriet will get the plane back to Chicago and Hadley the Boston flight to take her mother's place at Kate's bedside. My bus back to the city leaves Newark every hour on the half-hour.

Gardenia Cake

She isn't sure she'll survive the weekend. She tells us, "No one should have to go through what I'm going through."

It took so much just to complete the preparations, and she did it all herself. Drew up the guest list, figured out the seating arrangements for the dinner as well as the luncheon. She was on her feet all week last week checking out locations, it was hard on her back. But she laughs it off when I offer to give her a back rub. "Wrong sex!" she says cheerily.

The whole idea of a holding a symposium to celebrate her retirement was hers in the first place. She chose the topic and drafted the program, giving careful thought to the specialties of the speakers, what each one was likely to be most articulate about, their sensitive egos, then weighing her own interests and what she felt had been the direction of her career. She had to consider grant money too—if everything's phrased right some of the men can apply for funds from their departments or the government to reimburse them for travel expenses. That's how she and Alec manage to organize all those conferences they do together.

The guests spread out over the Great Lawn behind Languages following the closing afternoon session. Full professors and professors emeritus. Retired and active Episcopal priests from the local parishes and some from other parts of the state. The number eleven man from the Carter State Department accompanied by two diplomats who served in three administrations altogether, Democrat and Republican both. One Bishop Coadjutor. Heads of corporations and former heads. Ordinary businessmen who are members of the St. Ann's vestry, wives of people, widows. Town and country. A hundred guests sipping paper cups of champagne and nonalcoholic champagne. Maybe 150. Only the presence of the honoree herself makes sense of such a recipe of types—her "special touch," a speaker said at the luncheon.

She moves from group to group, pausing to shake hands or collapse into someone's embrace. A smattering of applause follows in her wake. A breeze rustles the cocktail dresses and lifts a few thin strands pasted over bald heads.

It's she who's brought them all together, who's kept things going, organizing them into committees, writing grant proposals and running conventions, inventing prizes, even winning some of them herself. At the final breakfast they plan to surprise her with a medal, newly minted, for Outstanding Contribution, to be awarded annually thereafter in her name.

The light declines behind the academic buildings. Can it be so late? What will they do without her? She mustn't retire.

But wait, there's news—a rumor on the breeze. Priest bends his head to poet, gray gabardine nudges pink silk. She isn't leaving them, she's only moving on. From strength to strength, as it were, in her new career as consultant she'll sit on boards, travel just as widely—advising, extending the frontiers. She won't let the causes she's nourished all these years wither on the vine, she won't let down her men. She'll be in even greater demand. Just this morning she had the cutest idea for a business card, she was talking about it, she says, with one of the daughters.

She just doesn't look like a widow, people tell her. Those bright, girlish colors, and the fashionable hemlines. She seems so young. The creamy skin. Her hair preserved in jet black.

Trailing behind her, thirty years younger, I feel every bit my age. I smoke too much, find crow's feet in my mirror. My own juices drying up. I ask my mother at what age she went through menopause but she doesn't remember. It must have started on the trip to Europe. Even she thinks I'm too thin—after a certain age, she says, it's not as attractive.

Between greeting so many guests she stops and fumbles in the pocket of her dress for a Kleenex. Dabs at her eyes. Blows her nose briskly to restore herself. How could she not be moved, seeing so many dear friends and colleagues? The meaning of her life spread out before her.

A third change of clothes and then the dinner given at the Valley Country Club by a family friend. Private room, white and gold table settings. My mother's pared the guest list down to thirty or so, intimates and family. She's asked Alec to act as master of ceremonies.

Gifts, toasts, bouquets. Behind-the-scenes anecdotes from long ago conventions—silly things the men did, the back-and-forth in hotel corridors, my mother keeping them all in hand.

Gerda, in her accent, raises a glass to the perfect faculty wife and hostess. She says Victor and Lillian always made her feel like a fourth daughter. Her hair's dark and shining with a new dye job. Saliva wets her teeth so the caps gleam.

Margaret, on behalf of the real daughters, presents our gift—a tiny soapstone sculpture of three polar bears, commemorating one of Lillian's favorite causes, the Inuits.

I toast my mother in song, verses in the tradition of Victor scribbled on the back of an envelope on my flight down and set to one of my mother's favorite tunes, "Where Have All the Flowers Gone?" The missing flowers are lilies. Mother's eyes fill at the reprise, which I sing in German ("Sag Mir Wo Die Blümen Sind?") as Joan Baez did it on a record that still sits on a shelf somewhere in Margaret's old room.

Wearing a blue silk dress that brings out her eyes, Clare rises, model thin, a typed tribute in her hand. She introduces herself as the fertile one. Caretaker and trustee of the next generation, Lillian's grandchildren—Marie, Charlotte, and John, the new baby. To them through her have passed her mother's many virtues and special talents. She nods left and right to the company like the gracious embassy hostess she's become. There are qualities she could only have inherited from her mother. Politeness, kindness, a sense of style. She reads on.

"Unfortunately, however, like my mother, I can't cook."

Laughter. Room sounds. The company settling back, ready to be amused.

Clare tells how when Victor asked his new bride to name her favorite dish, Lillian said "a saucer."

How Clare herself in her turn invariably burns the toast and lets the water boil away beneath Richard's breakfast eggs.

My mother laughs with everyone else, going along with it. In the changeable candlelight only a daughter would be able to detect the flicker of distaste in her eyes.

Could it be? She at whose table, in the larger sense, we're gathered this very night—Lillian a failure as a cook?

True, she came to her husband innocent and untutored. When he said *dish*, she thought *saucer*. When he called for his slippers, she asked, "Who was your nigger last year?" And he said, "Mia."

But she learned. She had to learn. Certain things were expected of a professor's wife. Right away she had to start giving dinner parties.

In the beginning Dad shipped them tins of sardines, anchovy paste, caviar, just the way he'd supplied the boys all those years ago at Princeton. Victor taught Lillian how to feel for a ripe avocado, he introduced her to artichokes. Twice she forgot about the boiling pot and they were hopelessly overcooked, the hearts tasteless. When they moved to Marshall he sent her for pastry-making lessons after work (she typed for Cornland Foods and Fertilizer) with the French *mamán* of a colleague in Romance Languages. They all became fast friends—Madame a surrogate European grandmother for Victor, Mademoiselle godmother to the new baby, Clare. They loved Madame's stories of life before the War in the little village outside Paris where her family had their chateau. They were blue bloods, related to royalty. She'd known Toulouse-Lautrec, "a nasty little man." She scolded Victor, much to his delight, and took pity on Lillian. No wonder she was nervous, with so many responsibilities to fulfill! No wonder she had spells! Madame sent her home, no matter how disastrous the results in class, with petits fours baked earlier in the day, ladyfingers for the Charlotte Russe Victor wanted served when they had the president of the College and his young third wife to dinner.

In North Carolina Lillian served southern fried chicken to the candidates who came down to interview for the Department. It was nice to give them a feeling for the region. She learned to cook turnip greens in the Southern fashion, soft and steamy. Saddlers was a family-style restaurant famous for its take-out barbecue and Brunswick stew—sometimes Victor swung by there with the candidate in tow before picking up Lillian from her office. Most Northerners had never heard of hush puppies, though a few years later you could buy them frozen—as good as homemade, one of Lillian's secrets.

There were luncheons for her secretaries, refreshments after monthly Wednesday night meetings when it was her turn to host her sorority. Dinners where Lillian tried to be creative with the guest list so faculty couples sat at the table with ordinary folk from Church. A woman told her, "I always meet such interesting people at your house."

There was Victor and Lillian's annual Tom and Jerry party on New Year's Day when they got to use Victor's grandmother's brass samovar, which otherwise sat on the dough tray in the dining room for decoration. Lillian polished it every year.

Who could question her reputation, her hospitality? It was why she stayed on in Victor's house after he died instead of moving into some cramped condominium like the other widows. She couldn't imagine living in a place where she couldn't entertain. What could Clare have meant?

If there were frozen dinners for the family, well, she had to work. She always worked, nine to five, rushing home to try and put something on the table Victor wouldn't find fault with so they could have a nice family dinner. If she hadn't worked, they wouldn't be here tonight— her dearest friends and colleagues gathered to honor her career.

If her daughters couldn't cook, if they didn't eat, that was something else. You have to choose to remember the good things.

Like the gardenia cake. It was so like her.

When we were teenagers, she baked a cake—maybe the mix came from a box, but what does it matter these days, she always said—and the middle fell through. She put it on a cake plate and frosted it anyway, with vanilla icing, then covered the hole with a gardenia blossom from the hundred-watt bush outside the kitchen door that Daddy tended on his way to and from the car. She retouched the frosting a little so none of it would look like a mistake and set the platter in the middle of the dining room table where otherwise in gardenia season she might float a single bloom in a bowl.

All through the house the scent of gardenia spread, unrolling like a tongue of white paint from a paint spreader, settling in the rooms and in the furniture.

The prettiness of the gesture, the whimsy, was a side of my mother my sisters and I knew mostly from stories—the early years of our parents' courtship and marriage, before any children came. The dish and the saucer. The time Victor booked a room at the Statler in Washington and arranged a rendezvous with his young wife while he was on leave. She got there ahead of him and ordered a drink from room service—"an Old Fashioned, make it a double"—using some phrase she'd heard from the movies. Imagine her surprise when two drinks came instead of one. And Victor's shock when he arrived to find his wife toasting Roosevelt with the bellboy—it seemed a shame to let the extra drink go to waste, she explained.

Gardenia flavor seeped from the petals into the white frosting and down through the pores of her cake so that when you ate it, you tasted the flower itself—more like an aftertaste really than a flavor.

It was a mistake the first time, after that she made it on request, whether or not the middle fell through, especially for me, she remembered years later. I liked foods with that sort of almond flavor—artichokes, avocados. All the *a* sounds. My father picked up one or the other when he went grocery shopping for my visits home from college or later from far-flung jobs as a temporary secretary or Poet in the Schools. Mother served the appetizer, and Daddy cooked filet mignon. He said I might not eat much but when I did I certainly had expensive tastes.

After I moved to New York I bought a gardenia plant every year. They appeared in flower shops around the beginning of March, shipped from Barbados. In the Yankee climate they had a precarious life span, at first needing every bit of the light in my tenement window then dying a parched death in a single day scorched by the summer sun. I had to start with a new one every spring. Sometimes it only managed to produce a single flower.

After ten years in the city, I feel like that struggling plant myself. A struggle to write, a struggle to eat. My nieces and nephew far away now in South America, I wander through a wintry Central Park, stopping at the sweeping Romantic statue of Robert Burns on his pedestal. His gaze is cast skyward, a scroll of paper falling from his hand with the flowing words of a poem inscribed there: MY MARY FROM MY SOUL WAS TORN . . .

At night I take the gardenia plant from the windowsill and set it on my bedside table so I'll be in the path of the powerful fragrance. I can't sleep anyway. Only that pungent gardenia beside me seems alive, its weight on the air heavy as cream, each blossom whipped into stiff scallops of frosting, uncurling from the glossy leaves like a note written on white paper and floated out to me on a glossy dark sea.

Point of View

Now I wish I could get out of it the prospect's got me so glum, it's not good to be around someone who's depressed, I should see Harriet though, you don't know how many more times you'll have, she's sending the neighbors to get me, I didn't say how long a layover it would be, maybe I'll call back, I think she'd come out to meet for lunch instead, you know those nice airport restaurants they have now, or a drink at a bar.

It's not really my family anyway, not what I came from, I should do something though.

You don't recover from those blows in life, no wonder she's not well, one right after the other, they say cancer of the liver's one of the worst ways but at least it was Frank's time, sometimes it's just your time, it's different watching a daughter, a daughter is one of the worst things, I know *I* couldn't.

I have to realize as you girls get older when one of you calls it could be about you.

I'm lucky, I'm one of those who never even had to watch a *parent* die.

Harriet had depression before you know, after the tuberculosis, oh yes, that first winter in Mexico, really crazy stuff if you ask me, a whole year without the plumbing in, that probably started it, they put her on something, I don't remember the names, Frank told Victor they had it under control.

Well, Hadley probably wouldn't have known the full extent would she, she already had her own life, a husband and children, people give a different version sometimes, you must know that from all your therapy, maybe she's loyal to her mother.

You thought Daddy was the one with the temper, Harriet didn't know what she'd taken on with Frank at first, the second wife rarely does, that marriage had a history let me tell you, it went way back.

Oh I know you had fun when he came to see us, you girls loved him, you loved those visits, I'm not saying he wasn't fun, he was very bitter though, always, you were too young to realize, it's a blessing really, we never said things in front of you.

Victor worried, the drinking and Frank's temper, then Mama moving in, he tried to mediate, he was very loyal to his brother you have to give him that, well, it could have happened to us, we were next, but then Mama had the stroke, I can't believe we managed to find a Christian Science practitioner in the Marshall phone book it was such a tiny place, that's when you asked me why doesn't Grandma believe in doctors when you can see them, we thought it was so cute, no you don't, you were too little to remember, you're just remembering the story.

People remember different things, your father always said wives and sisters-in-law could never keep the family stories straight no matter how often they heard them, that's part of what's depressing me I guess, the thought of going there just to sit around and analyze the past, they all do that, I don't think it's good for me at my stage, I need to look forward, it's just going to make me sad seeing her after all she's been through, I think a call from the airport's enough, I'm sure she'd love that.

Sunset

We followed Kate's husband, Will, into the woods out behind the houses where all the backyards met, smashing leaves under our sneakers. We stopped at the clearing.

Most of the trees were blown bare except for a few yellow flags hanging on here and there or a fiery sash at the waist. There were piles raked for burning. There was a cold wind, and the sun behind high thin clouds was a weak bulb so the light was smeared over the day.

One of the neighbors spoke, then Kate's best friend.

It was cold even through our sweaters, with the bars of sunlight blowing in and out that way, off and on, the property stripped to the ground—a whole season cremated.

Will told the two children what he hoped they'd always remember about their mother, the things she'd loved in each one, how she hadn't wanted to leave them.

Harriet and Hadley had said they couldn't speak. They asked me, as the representative of the North Carolina branch, to read something by each of the poets in the family.

I read my father's poem "Boys on the Island." I read a haiku by Uncle Frank I'd found in a letter in one of the boxes my mother was going through down in the study about the blue mountain in back of the house in Mexico. My hands shook the way they had when I read at Margaret's third wedding. I finished with my own poem to someone fair of face—it wasn't Kate, but it could have been. It could have been Clare, they had the same milky skin.

Will took the little tape recorder from his jacket and switched it on. Barber's *Adagio for Strings* started so slowly and quietly it seemed to be rising with the wind, stirring and lifting things from the ground.

Clicks from the pocket recorder and the sound of the tape stretching showed through the first measures.

The sun moved high in the branches behind the thin clouds, straining down.

Cello, violas, then the violins. The strings rose and rose again, piling up riches in that bare place, all it could hold.

We stood with our heads bowed waiting for it to stop.

The silence came up after it.

We turned to go.

Hadley grabbed me by the shoulders, and we kissed hard on the mouth the way the two old men, our fathers, had done. Tears ran down our cheeks. We locked arms on the walk back to the house over the crackling ground. The winter sun shone weakly through the absence of leaves, and the air was as milky as a fair sister's face.

Hadley told a dream Kate had a few days before she died. She said she saw her father swim out into the Gulf a little way and then turn back and wave. He called to her—come on, the water's wonderful.

But she told Hadley she thought not yet. She didn't want to go in just yet.

Harriet said most winter days the Gulf is as smooth as oil. After lunch they would turn the outdoor furniture around to face it. Then there were hours of discussion—between Frank and Harriet, Frank and whoever was visiting at the time—about the positioning and arrangement of the chairs, the most spectacular view, etcetera. It went on every afternoon. At last everyone took their places on the deck of the house in Mexico that Uncle Frank's retirement money had bought and watched as the sun sank into the water.

Eat & Excrete

She doesn't think she'll ever get used to it, how much garbage one person living alone can generate, don't you find yourself amazed being single, she asks me, the accumulation, it's as if she's always either on her way out to the garbage cans or coming back in, eat and excrete, that's all life is really.

Strange, because she watches her diet, coffee and unbuttered toast in the mornings, she's on the European plan as they say, yogurt and a piece of fruit for lunch, maybe one of those low-calorie TV dinners, they're really quite good now the way they make them and she's on a tight budget, it doesn't seem possible she's producing so much garbage.

She stopped buying those plastic garbage bags altogether, it's such a waste, why not use the same bag you brought the groceries home in, dump the scraps into that after you've eaten and take it right out, it's not so good when you think about it leaving garbage out, forcing people to look at it, it isn't that hard to clean up after yourself, why not have everything stay nice the way it was before?

She rinses her plate, silverware, and glass as soon as she's eaten and puts them right into the dishwasher so she doesn't need a dish rack beside the sink anymore either, it wasn't so great to look at it after all, why should everyone have to see everything?

Keep things tidy, that's what she believes in, that's why she put such time and effort into clearing out Victor's study, she can't live in a messy house, the kitchen's a constant battle, the refrigerator, the cupboards, a good rule is don't buy more than you're going to eat, when you use flour it's better to throw out whatever's left, just buy another bag the next time you need it, that way you discourage the weevils, she hasn't seen weevils in her kitchen since the three of us were teenagers.

I wake up unaccountably hungry in the middle of the night when I visit her and rifle through the cupboards just the way my father used to. I root out a jar of peanut butter behind the box of sugar and the unopened bag of flour. Maybe I should do as my mother keeps suggesting and move down here just to make myself desperate enough to eat. At home I force myself every day now to drink a six-pack of a nutritional supplement just to get the minimum number of calories. I'm trying everything—Prozac, therapy, a light-box. I've found an apartment on Long Island near the ocean.

Mornings, as soon as I come to, I pull on sweatpants and sweatshirt and head for the beach. Sit cross-legged on the sand and stare out at the waves, letting the pale sun warm me, the bad dreams melt away.

Tap tap tap
So early in the morning.

Sounds muffled by the lingering fog trying to reach me. Men banging on the sky. A construction site somewhere—there's always something new going up. The fog's like a veil between me and reality, a trance. Strange and familiar. Things half sensed . . . I watch the multitude of floaters on my retina climb the whitened sky . . .

Most things from the boxes in the study go in the discard pile, it gets bigger and bigger each time she really accomplishes something down here, my mother says, she stuffs those huge plastic garbage bags so full the drawstring won't pull tight and carries them outside, when there's no more room in the garbage cans she has to stack them next to the woodpile, it's embarrassing what the garbage man must think when he comes in the morning, when there's one of us there to help her we can fill up the trunk of the car and the backseat and drive down to the Church and use those giant bins outside the door of the parish house kitchen, no one's there to see us unloading in the dark.

Spider

Terrible, I didn't tell you? I thought I told you, I still have this awful dripping in my throat, makes me have to cough all the time, you can hear it can't you, can you hear it? Well, maybe it's the phone connection.

I should have canceled the thing for tonight but they were counting on me, the new person doesn't really know her way around yet and you know how helpless the professors are, someone has to see that Maintenance did the setup right and put paper and pencils beside each chair, people always forget, I had to check about the liquor too, you can't just have a couple of bottles of bourbon the way we do down here for a party you know, these men come from all over, they want scotch and gin, vodka, those young secretaries are a big help but they're sweet Southern girls, Baptist, they don't understand about professors and their drinking, they don't know the different types of liquor, and then there's the food table, people are at a loss where to go unless someone directs them, they all stand in a huddle around the speaker, I don't know what it is.

Well, it went fine, of course, I managed to bring the whole thing off, I think I may have done something to my back though, it was aching so, I was on my feet the whole time, you know how those men go on and on, even after they broke up I had to stand there listening, I took my temperature as soon as I got home.

Normal, it's completely normal now, in fact it's below normal, is that a bad sign? I'm used to my temperature being right at normal,

I'm still taking the antibiotic you know, what? Oh yes, he had to call something in for me.

I don't know, something-mycin, you know I never remember those things, Daddy was always the one, you're just like Daddy, you want me to go look? I could always go look.

I have to be careful now when I get something, living alone, it could turn serious overnight and there wouldn't be anyone here, this could have turned into pneumonia for all we know if I hadn't phoned the doctor, just last week Mary Evans was diagnosed with walking pneumonia, her daughter had to take her in.

Well, it's a serious problem for people like me, their health, you should pay attention too, there's a danger with women living alone, widows and old maids, it's important to have someone who can check on you now and then, I worry about your moving way out there on Long Island away from all your friends, you remember the terrible thing that happened with Dorothy Fletcher.

You don't remember? I didn't tell you? It must be over a year by now, you do remember Dorothy Fletcher, Dottie, Miss Fletcher, she was secretary to the Classics Department all those years, she had to take early retirement of course, she was always so fond of you girls, so sweet, I think she found some information for you once when you needed help with your Latin, remember? You brought home a B and Daddy wanted to hire his graduate student to tutor you.

Well, she was a special lady, I felt so sorry for her, that terrible birthmark all the way across the bridge of the nose, I don't know why she never got them to remove it, they can take care of things like that nowadays you know, it's just a procedure.

I felt bad I never went to see her that last year, no really sometimes I'm almost ashamed, I see the things the other widows are doing, Mary Wright driving people to their chemotherapy, letting the families stay at her house overnight, I'm not like that, I couldn't do it, I just have to contribute in my own way I guess, all my conference work, world population growth and the rest, I guess you could say I've given.

I did see her that last time before she got the diagnosis, Dottie,

Miss Fletcher, it was at the Bevan funeral, you knew he died didn't you, you remember Dick Bevan, now there was an untimely death.

All the old people from the Classics Department showed up, the old Classics Department, even the DiStephanos, they're both still alive you know, the wife's in terrible shape now, just terrible, he had to help her down the aisle, it was so sad, he's not very steady himself, feeble really, remember how handsome he was? I always thought Dottie was secretly in love with him, she carried a torch all those years typing for him, not that she ever would have said anything, she'd have been mortified to think anyone even suspected, people knew though, people always know.

I think she would have gotten married and had a normal life if she'd had that birthmark removed, there was someone in her past you know, she told me in confidence once, a young man who died, she never got over it really, then she had to spend all those years taking care of an infirm mother, that's the Southern tradition though, by the time her mother died Dottie was middle aged, just another middle-aged spinster, that's a hard life you know.

All those things they say about women who never marry? She said it was true, she told me she used to plan little treats for herself, things to get herself out of the house once or twice a week, ask some of the widows she knew to go out to eat with her or go to the movies, she used to take herself to a movie every week, she said she didn't mind it sitting there all alone.

I'm telling you some of them end up alcoholic, they don't even bother to cook for themselves after a while, they'll sit down to have one or two drinks at night and pretty soon they think why not have a third or a fourth, why go to all that trouble fixing dinner when there's no one to fix it for.

Such a sad ending, even for her, I'd never heard of anything like it before, I kill spiders right and left when I'm cleaning, you know how we get them down here overnight in the bathrooms with their webs no matter how often you clean it gets so muggy but now honestly I'm afraid to, I'd just as soon wait till one of the other girls is here with her husband, Black Widows I knew, of course, that's just something that comes with the South when you move down here, those don't live inside, my men in Forestry reassured me about that, but this is different, these will come right in, you never know, you could brush against a web by accident and get bitten, right inside your own house, "Brown Recluse Spider," I never even knew the term.

It was the symptoms that finally got Dottie to get herself checked, it doesn't take long they tell me, paralysis can set in in less than twenty-four hours and then there's nothing anyone can do, by the time she got to them there wasn't a thing the doctors could do for her.

So sad, a tragedy really, you know the phrase Southern Gothic, not even time to say good-bye to anyone, not that Dottie had anyone to say good-bye to, poor thing, just another lonely old maid, it's a sad commentary when there's no one to hear your last words.

Well, there's a lesson there I'm sure, how important it is to go in for regular checkups, I'm sure Dottie avoided going to the doctor as much as possible, spinsters are like that, they're very shy about undressing in front of a doctor, gynecologists especially, you can imagine what kind of torture that was for her, really, it's a well-known fact, you put off appointments year after year and then end up with cancer of the uterus, vagina, whichever it is, your chances are double or triple I think, I read an article, especially if you've never had children.

I hope *you* go to the gynecologist regularly, you do have a gynecologist don't you?

Well, I thought I'd ask, I didn't know if you've found new doctors at the beach or if you still go to your old ones on the days you're in the city, you have a regular doctor don't you, it's important to have someone who actually looks at your body once in a while.

We have to stop now, really, I worry about your money, I'm glad this came up about the medical appointments though, I've been meaning to talk to you, I must say I've gotten very good about it now that I'm a widow, I do make the effort, you have to, you have to pay attention, this whole thing with my nose and throat could have gone right to the chest if I hadn't been careful, you can never tell when a symptom could be a sign of something.

I'm tired

I'm tired of waking up
at the crack of dawn
High tide

smelling near

freighted with sighs
full of dreams
saved up for breakfast

Stormy
Dishevelled
Tossed
Stirred up from under

Barefoot on the creaking boards
Swaying
Braced
Cheeks slapped awake
His head anointed

(It can't be
It didn't happen
It's like coming to the ocean
In the middle of Iowa)

Anniversary

It's easy to get those dates mixed up, she says, she must have been
looking at the wrong month on her calendar, maybe she had on her
other pair of glasses.

She likes to take something there to put on the grave, it looks so bare otherwise, Mr. Spender next to him always has fresh flowers, his wife's out there every week, well, Victor was no tobacco baron, he didn't leave her a fortune to squander at the florist's, a plant's a nice idea don't you think, something that lasts longer than just one Sunday to the next.

Father Tom says The Prayer for the Departed and reads out the list of Faithful Servants, and she crosses herself at Victor's name then has to fumble behind her glasses where the tears have risen suddenly.

It's done automatically, the Church secretary keeps a file, it's all computerized now of course, if Father Tom's called to another parish or when he retires the new man will know whom to pray for when, generations will hear the names of the founding families, they print them in the program that's mailed the week before an anniversary, that's always a reminder.

She likes to donate the altar flowers for the Sunday of the anniversary, after the service they go to whoever's in the hospital, it's a gesture that means so much, you never know whose time it is, her budget's so tight it doesn't seem too much to ask the three of us to go in on it with her even if we won't be in town.

One year she went up there at the cocktail hour, she found that old flask of Victor's, they used it on car trips remember, and she drove to the Church and poured herself a jigger sitting on his grave, well, standing, they don't like to find the widows slobbering on their husband's graves, it was her little joke, then at the end she poured a little on the ground, a splash of bourbon to warm his bones, he would have liked that.

He might have lived you know, she has lots of friends who've made it to their nineties, people live a long time now.

She pours a third drink, a toast to his memory, it's nice when one of his girls is home to celebrate with her even if it's not the exact date, it's whenever we're together that's what counts, he'd understand, the important thing is to remember.

"Where was I?"

The wonderful opportunities, the scholars and musicians from all over the world he brought into this house.

She knew what was going on, people said things to her, she wasn't fooled for a minute.

It's dark down in the family room where she holds court, she has to save now on the electric bill, just the one lamp at the far end of the sofa where she sits with her stocking feet curled under her, rubbing the instep of one foot over the top of the other, making that sound, and the lick of the green and yellow flame from the starter log, darker still at the Church half a mile down the road where they've turned off the floodlights for the night and locked and bolted the doors to the sanctuary, and out in the cemetery it's dark, darker under the earth where my father lies, it's solid dark.

But things happen in the dark, even in death they're changing, it happens to all of us, death's a part of life, you learn to accept it, we all go on.

Underground his bones return the last strains of calcium, the line of his lip slackens, he can't argue.

What good is his temper now, muffled by clods?

She thought he might say something at the end, maybe he'd apologize.

She lifts her chin and holds it there: a simple request.

All her requests were simple, she came to him from simple people, her good mother, her plain father, it was Victor who took everything and turned it around, her words, her life, who twisted everything.

He wooed her with his poems, he said Jay would never be able to give her an intellectual life, it's true, of course, he was just a simple farm boy.

Her mouth curls at the bitter taste of what she's forced to say.

Once upon a time, a long long time ago, it was too late.

Well, at least she's getting it off her chest, that's important, it's important to have someone listen to your troubles now and then.

TEACHER, POET, TRANSLATOR she made sure his epitaph read the way he'd dictated it to her—or did she get the order wrong?

167

It/Him/It
Stalled like a front

Riding over the line

Breathing uneasily
Out of season
Heated

And always searching
the borders like that

Bobbing and
nodding on top

Squalls
Fits and starts

Heading in
then tacking

Back-tracking
Head-faking

Trying to shoulder his way past

Lord of All

She wants that same hymn they used for Daddy, you know the one, she tells me, something-something hopeful, from the Randall Jarrell funeral, remember? When *was* that? They drove all the way to Greensboro.

Daddy knew all those guys, she says, Ciardi, Jarrell, they were in the magazines together, you children met them when you were babies, everyone came through Marshall to read at the College, they never forgot the three little girls, the wives would ask about you in their Christmas cards, Shapiro's the only one left now, if he's still alive, that's the kind of thing you could probably find out on the Internet.

Victor really was someone in his day you know, remember when you were a teenager and he inscribed a copy of his second book for you "to the better poet"? That was something coming from a father like him.

"Lord of all hopefulness," . . . yes, that's it, oh Wendy, you still have that lovely voice, she says, it's a shame you don't use it, there must be choirs on Long Island, won't you play it for her after lunch, she'll just bring down a few pieces of fruit after the salami, no one's touched the piano in so long.

It would make a nice recessional don't you think, something to lift the congregation's spirits, a funeral's a celebration in our Church you know, of the person's life, people should remember what she was to her family and her community not the fact that she's gone.

She's just about got all the hymns now, it's the order she needs to work on, then she'll choose the Special Prayers.

Well, it's something to think about while she's sitting through that long service by herself.

Father Tom has such a lovely voice doesn't he, Southern but not too, the way they talk around Sanford where he's from, it goes so well with the prayers, our lovely Anglican liturgy, well you grew up with the *old* prayerbook, the *old* liturgy, that was the real thing, this generation doesn't even remember.

Tom can be quite profound sometimes actually, people don't expect it from him, it's not what they want in a sermon, they don't want to be made to think, it's their day off, they want to sit in the pew with their families, you can understand, they work hard, those executives, people don't realize.

It's such a nice view through the side windows, you can look right out at Victor and the others, the grass growing over them, sometimes she

169

lets her mind wander, well, you could spend the whole service every Sunday just looking at the stained glass window behind the altar and not run out of things to think about in those biblical scenes, you knew he died didn't you? The artist? The famous one? You knew a famous Italian artist designed the big stained glass window, didn't you? Whew, she thought for a minute you didn't know about the famous window, remember, they had it on display in Grand Central Station in Washington first, that's right Union Station, they shipped it over from Italy in pieces and reassembled it, then they had to take it apart again and put it back together down here, people come from all over.

She likes how Jesus looks as if he were watching you, such sad eyes.

Like the eyes in that old poem of Daddy's, remember? You saw Jesus out the kitchen window in Marshall and he wrote about it, you must have been in your highchair then, you thought Jesus was walking across the top of the honeysuckle hedge.

You'll come with her tomorrow won't you, as long as you're down here, have you seen the little plaque yet with Victor's name on it on the family's old pew? Well, it's not the exact same pew, she couldn't be sure about that, but it's in the general area, back in the back where we always had to sit because he got us there so late.

It was expensive, real gold is, it took her over a year to pay for it, she had to cut down on her regular pledge, of course you girls helped with your contributions, she says, Margaret especially.

Pledges are way down, people don't donate the way they used to, Father Tom confided in her, they don't tithe anymore, she's always tithed, but then she's not one of the ones who can make the really big contribution, you have to rely on corporate people for that, they pull down such enormous salaries you know, people like her friend from Duke Power, you remember that nice man, the old-timers are good about it actually, it's the younger generation she faults, they've never developed the habit, it's a different set of values, it's not how they live, a lot of them have moved here from the North.

It's good for the Church though, so many new people coming now, young couples with children, you can't keep a parish going if you don't bring in the next generation.

She hates to wake me in the morning knowing how late it always is when I switch off my light, maybe you could make a special effort, she says, so you won't look so tired the next day, she likes to get there early for the music, it's Holy Communion, I don't mind do I taking an old lady to Church, it means something to her, people are always asking about her girls, they're our family too really, they only get to see us once or twice a year now.

Body & Blood

I like to think about the Body and the Blood. I like to sit there with her year after year on Christmas Eve through that long Communion service at midnight mass in the same back pew, the one they named for him, and count the rows of people ranked in front of me, shoulder to shoulder, Christian soldiers, so straight and true, old families and the new, I like to line them up in my sights.

While down in front the priest raises the Host in the name of the Almighty, lowers it, raises the chalice, praises Him high and low, opens and closes his snowy wings.

Me too, I like to study the famous stained glass window behind the altar and trace the ruby drip of Precious Blood all the way down then turn to the other window on our right and gaze out at the founding fathers, Victor and the other old men plotted row on row, their borders trimmed neat.

I watch the new old families file in, long-haired boys from my Sunday School class now middle-aged fathers escorting their own children into the pews where their parents sat, widows on the arms of middle-aged sons led to the front rows where they can hear more, see more, by addition or subtraction of the flesh I can find their old faces.

I like to think about the suicides, I like to call the roll in my mind, the ones you don't count, the kid who got his first car and drove it into the first bridge abutment he could find, the spouse wheeled in every Sunday, whose name gets named when we say the Prayer for the

Afflicted, so brave and true, crimped in her chair, struck down by one of those, you know, pick one, degenerative muscular things, she gets home delivery of the Sacrament when she can't make it, she takes it by intinction directly on the tongue because her hands shake too much, her head lolls, she has no other hope but she manages, rolling in on holidays a tremulous example to us all, and we take it in the face, in the eyes and the teeth, smiling, because we have no brains, no real hearts, we're all just so polite.

And the priest's hand comes out of his robes and he places it on the lolling head and gives her Absolution.

Then one night, I think it was a Saturday, there was Church the next morning, or maybe it was Christmas Eve, anyway they were planning to bring her in, but she searched and found the family gun, loaded, hidden in the bosom of the family, a closet in the family room, I don't know how she got in there by herself but I guess she managed, and she stuck it in her mouth and pulled off a round, and Mercy flowed out the other side at last.

I like to remember the elders, the grandmothers and the great-grands counting out their last days in hospital beds at University Hospital until their Maker shall see fit, who finally got tired of waiting and ripped out the whole mess of tubes and plugs and waved it under your noses and died laughing.

I think about how you shoveled dirt in their mouths, how smoothly you sealed everything over and seeded the ground.

You range all around me, row on row, shoulders squared in rectitude, your lips ope'd in holy O's.

> Now my tongue the mys-t'ry tell-ing
> Of the glorious Bo-dy sing . . .

The God-made-flesh. Dwelt the seed of truth to sow.

I drift along the vaulted ceiling at the cornices and dream of severing the tongues of the gargoyles and watching them snake down the aisle to climb the polished sides of the pews and into your laps, hissing and wagging with the Good News, the True Word.

172

I could take you all out with one blast from behind my eyes.

But your ranks are so true, so plumb and square, there's no way, there never was, you know how to keep it going year after year, verse after verse, Christmas after Christmas. *Family, family, family.*

Grandmother's House

She's gotten practically religious about it, every evening after supper up to the Church and back, sometimes she keeps on going and takes the long way through the woods behind the house, it's important, something she can pass on to her daughters maybe, now that we're all getting older, sort of a tradition, the value of staying in shape going into these last years.

She does miss a day now and then, that's why having the grandchildren for these months is so good, it pushes her to do things, she takes them with her, you know the playground at Church, they have everything there now, a swing set, well, it's something she can do for the family.

Clare's a wonderful mother to those children no wonder she's thin, she has to think up something every minute to keep them entertained, they expect it, if they were in their own house they could go to their separate rooms, well, soon enough, she has her fingers crossed, Richard says the new stateside job should be permanent, if she can help out while he's tying things up in Caracas what grandparent wouldn't, how many get that chance in their lifetime watching a third generation grow and change before your eyes?

She feels better having them sleeping in the house anyway, it's not such a smart idea necessarily someone her age alone every night, something could happen.

And the two girls have been very good really, they straighten up after themselves, they don't tear around like rowdy children, she did know to put things away, the china and the glass ornaments she likes to have on display, especially now with John walking.

She loves having them with her on Sundays at Church, her friends love seeing them dressed up, John in the jacket she bought him and those cute little trousers, he keeps trying to roll the cuffs up to his knees and out of the way, but the girls enjoy the dress-up part, those two spend hours trying on their different clothes, they get restless sometimes when she has people over but they speak very nicely to adults, she gets compliments, only Marie once in a while, she has opinions, she doesn't understand we don't always need to say them out loud.

Certain things she can't help speaking to them about, habits they've picked up somewhere, language, from their friends probably, she'd be remiss if she didn't.

She tries to help with their table manners but they don't seem to be interested.

Well, they're not her children what can she do, you can't spend your last days worrying about your children's children and she wouldn't want to alienate Clare, she made that vow when they first talked about this arrangement, people have their own way of doing things, every family works out its own life, she's always respected that.

John does have a temper, she can't help noticing, it's not a good sign at such a young age, barely two, no matter what you tell him he shakes his head *no*.

And there's too much television in the house, someone should speak to Clare about that, we know now what it does to children, all that violence and sex so far ahead of time, they should be outdoors, they're missing their childhoods, well there's her walk, at least that's something she can do so they're not parked in front of that set morning, noon, and night turning into little zombies.

Just go on without her, she says.

Really.

Go.

She can't leave everything like this just to take a walk and then have to face it all when she comes back, it's not a question of help, no, it's better if she deals with it alone, people know their own dishwashers, where to stack things so the jet hits directly and particles of food aren't left stuck to the sides of the plate or scum inside the glasses.

No, no one said anything, of course not, not that she heard at any rate, she's allowed to change her mind once in a while isn't she, it was while we were upstairs getting sweaters, besides she doesn't pay attention to the girls when they're being silly, feelings can't be hurt at her age, let's hope John doesn't copy his sisters now that he's starting with words.

Watch it.

Too much back and forth with the swinging door, everyone helping at once, just leave things on the table where they are, there's no room left in the kitchen, it must be the extra plates she had to bring Marie and Charlotte so they could pick the onions out of her meat loaf, she'll put in a load first then get the rest herself, she can do it alone if she makes a lot of small trips.

Go.

We can manage the children by ourselves this once can't we? Why should it be one of *us* who misses out on the nice light?

No need to feel bad for her, she took a walk after all, a very nice walk thank you, it was while the rest of us were gone, she says, she thought we might be curious to hear, Marie and Charlotte especially.

She was doing the dishes when the side bell rang and there was a knock at the kitchen door, two little girls exactly their ages, eight and ten, wasn't that something, they wanted to know if she'd walk with them up to the Church and back it was such a fine evening, they were so polite, she couldn't say no.

Clare says we would have seen them, but she shakes her head no, they were having such fun they didn't stop at the Church after all, they kept on going the long way down the road behind the house and back around to the end of the driveway where they said good-bye.

Oh there was plenty of time, they made good time, they were practically skipping, she can't remember skipping in so long you'd think she would have forgotten how.

Where do they live then, Clare asks, those two strange little girls, and she says it's in the neighborhood somewhere, a house, down the block a ways, they pointed to it in passing, white with green trim, one of those.

So Clare rises from her chair, she'll take her own two girls to see them then, won't it be nice having someone their own age so close by to play with while they're here.

Oh no. Mother jumps up to stop her. They weren't staying, they were visiting some people in the neighborhood, they had to go back to their own home right away, those two little girls.

She takes a bobby pin from her hair and opens it with her teeth.

Maybe she'll go up and get ready early, she has that wonderful new biography that's been keeping her awake reading half the night.

Doesn't the television program the girls like to watch start about now?

Wendy, maybe you can help your sister by taking the girls downstairs while she puts John to bed.

Later when we tuck Marie and Charlotte into the twin beds in our old room and kiss them goodnight, Charlotte asks shouldn't we search the neighborhood in the morning just in case. But Clare says no, remember, she explained it to them, what happens sometimes with older people.

Charlotte's eyes are wide, hypnotized by tiredness or with what she's imagining—those two other little girls coming up the steps to her grandmother's kitchen and ringing the bell so politely, her grandmother opening the door to them. They must have worn their best Sunday dresses they look so nice. Not a spot on them.

Gray
Yellow
Pink

Faint
stains

176

Clicks and starts

A deep breath drawn

in the slack
before the pause
breaks up
and the salt cliffs detonate

Skin, Eyes, Teeth

There's some loss of hearing at every age, even you girls, she says, at your stage of life, your hearing's not as acute as when you were children, she read an article.

And then so many people mumble, particularly younger people, Victor was right about that, they never take the trouble to speak up, that new young priest they've brought in to assist at Church, well he's middle-aged really, you girls' ages, she says, once a month he gives the sermon and there are times she actually has to lean over and ask her neighbor in the next pew what it was all about so she can make some reference to the content the way she likes to after the service when he's shaking hands at the door and her turn comes.

Mike's the one who arranged to have her tested for the hearing aid, he's always been a good friend to the family, she can confess her troubles to *him*, he has the knowledge besides and not just in his own narrow medical discipline, she'd hate to miss hearing his beautiful baritone when the choir processes down the aisle.

It protrudes a little from the shell of her ear but she can't afford one of the smaller models, even with this one it's going to take her quite some time to finish making the payments, she just has to keep at it every month, and then you're supposed to replace the batteries once in a while, that alone is an expense.

What choice does she have though really, so many people

depending on her, conferences all over the country, board meetings, government grant applications she helps write, she's as busy as she ever was when Alec was alive, what? she asks. She didn't tell me? It was over a year ago, he was in Africa she heard, some kind of jungle fever, oh yes he died.

She has plenty of other suitors though, everyone's always trying to fix her up, the other widows from Church, faculty wives, they feel uncomfortable having an unattached woman at their dinner parties, it's understandable, usually she's seated next to one of the community's longtime bachelors, that's what they used to call them anyway and really she thinks maybe that's what they *were*.

There's a widower from the faculty, some professors do outlive their wives believe it or not, he squires her to concerts, he even brought flowers to her door once, she can't say no, it would hurt his feelings but she tries not to encourage him.

It's too much for one person really, she's going to start cutting back on some of the traveling, running up and down the country, it's not good to spend so many hours in the air, it hurts her ears, they say it's a hazard to the entire laryngeal system.

And all those hotel rooms, always the same old thing, she'd rather be in her own house where she's comfortable, surrounded by the things she knows, the people, her little route back and forth to the campus, the grocery store, Church, the Medical Center, they have all her records and you won't find better doctors anywhere in the world, that's one thing she's learned in her travels.

She tries to pass on some tips to us, proper care applied to the teeth and gums so you don't end up with so many problems, they're the only teeth you'll ever have, and skin requires extra moisture as it ages, she recommends keeping a bottle of lotion beside you at work or at home when you're doing chores, deterioration begins in middle age but at least you can do something to retard the process.

New thicknesses are added to her glasses, further distances between herself and the world.

Those last few years when she and Alec would meet they tried to overlook the physical changes, she says, they'd reached that stage of life when you learn to be kind.

She turns off the ring on the phone now when she's down in the study working, why make herself nervous with the jangling, people will always call back and she doesn't need a ring does she if she wants to call out, or in the evening in the family room if there's a program on television, not that she watches that much television, she's never been interested really, that's a difference between the generations, ours and hers, not to mention the grandchildren, she wouldn't want to count the hours they spend.

When she's dressing to go out, she may not even put the hearing thing in, it's so much trouble and really she gets along quite easily without it, she managed perfectly well at that last party she thought, the one with the Arabians, or when one of us comes to visit, why bother if we're sitting together in the family room over drinks or coffee after dinner like this, why waste the juice, it just means having to replace the battery that much sooner, you'd be surprised how much a tiny thing like that can cost, she really doesn't *need* a hearing aid when all she's going to do is talk.

> *The sea lifts the boat*
> *the boat pins the sea*

Spillville

It's never over, it keeps on happening, the tale unspooling from her tongue, anything might come up, I can't tell how it turns out.

Her hearing takes her farther and farther away, I don't know when I have her attention or when I don't, if I ask a question she may answer something else or not at all, my own words come back to me, warped and bent, there are baffles in the atmosphere, shuddering wings as though a moth flew into the ear canal and got trapped there—but is it my ear or hers? It's not her fault, I can't hear myself either, I don't know what I might say.

Wait for me, Mother, don't leave me in the dark, don't go, don't subtract yourself from me, sans ears, sans eyes, don't back down, don't wear away, don't start running out, don't let them retire you piece by piece until you're down to something they can manage, a whimpering thing, like him, in the hospital crib, a bother they have to turn first on one side then the other, don't reach for me, don't lean on me to steady your steps the way he did, leave me my cold eyes, leave me at least my stone heart—

Why must I bury the parents who buried me?

What did you say? Wait, I can't keep up, there's a blank spot where I wasn't paying attention, now a whole section's missing and I have to feel my way, blinders at either side, holes in everything, spots in front of my eyes, and then that fluttering comes again, the limp, limp sound of his wings—I think he's dying in there.

I reach out but I can't get a grasp, it all falls away when I reach for it, you said fine like you didn't notice, everything's fine, but each time you said that it went farther away.

A soft touch, full of woe, it's so sorry but it can't.

What's your face doing, what is that, why does it look that way, what do you mean, your mouth pulled down at one corner, eyes wide and roving, everything bending and stretching, it feels so ill, is that what meaning looks like, is that what meaning *means*?

There's a lapse where the eye rolls up, an ellipsis, a slack in this very sentence, there's nothing going on here now, it can't be expressed, that's why they can't find us, trapped in a time lapse, my eyes are so fogged, no outlook, just this hole where someone breathed on the glass, that's where I look, the mouth hole, I watch what comes out there . . .

You say "in life," you say "things happen in life," but I know it's not true, I know it's but a dream, fish-mouthed words and a bulging eye, the drag of the atmosphere pulling you down—

Please don't say anything more, Mother, I can't watch, I see the worm dripping from your lip, I know you mean me.

It's a spell, isn't it, there's a spell over everything, you know what that's like, first that funny thing happens with your vision, then a split, a tearing, you say you're fine, everything's fine, you put some other words there in place of what happens, things are what you say they are, but the body says different, my body hurts, it's a map, there's a map drawn there, printed on the body so we grow up that way, listing to the left or right, some of us our whole lives, pulled down on one side, moving according to some instruction we've forgotten long ago, steered by a zombie, felled by a stroke, one whole side of us uncooperative, out of commission . . .

Something comes over me, something comes down over me and takes possession of my body—

Mother, I think all my life I've been trying to remember something.

She gives it to me on a plate, she puts it right in front of me but I won't, I can't, I never have.

Don't make me, don't force me, I can't listen anymore, I can't take anymore in, I'm not a container you can use and reuse again and again, it won't all fit, my head will split, if I have to take just one more thing, I'll spit it right back out, I'll spill, I'll spew.

I'm her listener, I put myself there, I place myself in her pathway, the stream of her words, me, the double-crossing daughter, the traitor from up North, the literary one, you know, she can tell *me*.

And I'm down for it, I'm in for the sting—a word here, a nod—I can make anything happen, she can't defend herself, she doesn't know what she might say.

Mother, I'm not nice like you, I don't have your nice skin or your charm, your kind mother, your retiring father, your queue of male admirers. I'm not loyal, I have no pride, no shame, I live to bring us down.

I'm the woman you warned me against, the spidery spinster, two drinks before dinner and then why not make it a third, why bother to set the table, nothing to cook, no one to come home to, the cupboard's bare, it doesn't even taste like food anyway.

No dinner, no husband, no child, every night like clockwork I go out to watch the sun set, I'm just a spiny piece of driftwood pushed along the beach.

Orange, purple, pink, spilling down, spreading out over the water, your dire warnings, your predictions, putt-putt clouds and great swatches—you wrote it so large—it's indelible, isn't it, my fate, you can't rinse away the whole sky.

(This light's so strange I think it's going to seize, I think something's going to happen, yellow-green tornado light like back in Iowa, a light held down by only a few trees.)

> I want men, Mother
> North and South,
> with my fingers
> with my mouth

It's so dark though I'm afraid, I don't know what comes next, getting harder for me to walk now, Mother, I keep bumping into things I can't feel, harder to talk, harder to say what's happening, move the lips, lift the tongue, what if I just blurt something out, what will you do, what if I start to bleat and moo, will you shut me up, will you put me away, will you leave me there?

Mother, when a woman leaves me it hurts all over, in my chest and along my arms, in my knees, my feet, it's like a door slammed in my face, a truck ran over me, I feel like a bad accident, I'm dead or she is, why does my body hurt so, then losing sensation, then ghostly, just a scrap of something left, a leaf scrap, a skittering shell, some kind of refuse, I want to throw it away.

Tap tap
Rattle-trap

Teeter-totter

The floor looks up
when the door comes in
Side to side
but it can't be found

Something behind
Coming around

What's happening, Mother, what happened, you've got to say, there's a missing piece, time's running out, there's a hole and the seconds are leaking, I'm all in pieces, we have to stop talking now, the session's over.

Put your hand against my forehead, hold me back, the words come pouring out, chunks like books—

All over everything.

It's Spillville time, Lillian, I'm going to spill, spill all over your ville, I'm out, I'm letting go, leaving my house, my walled-in life behind, I'm going to beachcomb, going to catch the setting sun, it drops like a slot piece, red and swollen, into the ocean—I'm going to bring it right back up.

It's loud out here, Mother, it's all boomers and bangers, far-off thunder cliffs, boomers taking headers, dunderheads butting and rebutting, a shore ground out under tremendous pressure, detonation, reverberation, cuffs and blows, Teutonic sounds sending up spray like a host of galleon wings—ghostly sails, a ship, *Mother, I see something out there.*

Horned like a shrimp trawler, bucking the tide, moving and staying, toiling like a hydrofoil, listing from side to side with the pull of the nets.

Freighted, weighted, dripping with entanglements.

A masterpiece replete with masts and sails, groaning and complaining, stung with salts, swabbed with ointments, leaking calcium—

I'd know him anywhere.

Marooned between the Old World and the New, pitching and tossing and churning up the waters, roiling surf and thunderclouds like the ones in the old boiling paintings hung in the great museums he took us to all across the Continent.

Tintorettos and sunset tints.

Look, Mother, rising from the water, Hydra-headed, shedding iridescent scales, Argus-eyed, a sly periscope tracking our shores—

That groaning, shitting old man, that child-changed father.

Dipping his nets, lifting his weeping sheets strung with weeds and barnacles.

He's scraping the bottom, he's bringing up everything, he's lifting us all in his arms.

Him, It, Him treading his slick, spreading out his train, grooming himself—his garment, his raiment, his wake beaten into gold.

> Armor
> Shield and
> Dumbstruck flashback

I know his story, I have the art to reckon his groans.

Mother, the sky's so pale, so thin, a membrane stretched to its limit, I think it's all going to separate now along this line, my sight's cracking open, first a split, then a tearing, I see the cells streaming upward—

I can see inside the structure of things.

Bring me paper, Mother! Bring me a pencil!

Undoing the Spell

Tap tap tap
So early in the morning

Seesaw

Gray
Yellow
Pink

Faint
stains

Signed on smoke

(*Ashes, ashes*
My sacrifice
is so fragrant)

So much sky, even the ocean is a sky. The mist like a veil, the world behind the world . . .

I hug my knees to my chest, brush the sand like bits of eraser from my notebook page.

Everything penciled in, so tentative, thin, unsteady, drizzling wires, antennas, wobbly as fawn legs, a fawn finding its legs, *teeter-totter* . . .

The mist evaporating, a fine rain, *tick, tick, tick*, the drizzling air like a needle on a phonograph record, it picks up a scratch and rides it, over and over.

The pot has a little hole in it

Round and round.

Drizzle, puzzle, the floaters & motes in my vision, I watch them swim upstream against the sky, heads or tails . . .

>Blurred heads with
>Streaming tails
>Threads
>
>Things with legs
>Finding their legs
>
>Antics
>Swimming tricks
>Mistakes
>
>(Hand
>over hand
>bar by bar
>hope climbs the ribcage)

Who figured the grid for this? The sky has hooks and ladders you can climb, platforms, rigging, *the sky's rigged, the whole sky's rigged.*
Versions and gestures caught in the crosshairs.
Tap, tap, tap. A high-wire act.
Who's that? Who's in back? What's behind the scenery? Tap, tap, tapping till the mists drift, the drifts part, the surface tension unzips like Velcro splitting . . .
A gap, a gasp, and then the panels of the sky swing open . . .

>*Tap, tap, realitat-tat*
>Inset
>Insects
>Alive inside
>
>Centipede details

Eyes on stilts
Men on Legs

Swarming
scrambling
spawning

Crawling

All over
everything

There are men behind the sky, behind the flimsy membrane, tapping
and tapping, trying to get through to me, *I always knew it*, distant
hammers, tiny figures, climbing and clamoring.

Caution
Men at Work
Men banging on the sky

Over here. In the upper righthand corner. They're setting up a
structure. *Tap, tap*, elevated tracks, a lattice.
Suspension bridges, declensions . . .
Like diagramming sentences.
You have to parse each part as though you're just learning to read.

Compound-complex

2-by-4's
laid end to end

& perpendicular

Transitive
Intransitive

A bucket left dangling

Teeter-totter

A bit of tin
Wincing

Oil refineries, long-legged spiders extruding silk, toiling microbes under the magnifying lens of quiet, their spidery handwriting an insubstantial framework, melting, coming back, in-and-out reception . . .

Gray
Yellow
Pink

dawning &
fading
& melting like candy

Tap, tap, who's that? So early in the morning. What do you want? Tapping and tapping on the bones of my ear (*hammer, anvil, stirrup*). Dot, dash. *Rik-tikki-tik*. Uneasy meanings. Prickling misgivings. Under my skin.

Eyes front
Eyes on Legs
Men setting foot on the sky

Light-fingered, stealing over the surface, tap, tap, tapping like a blind man going over an elephant.

Seesaw go the saws, the sawdust rising, turning the air pink.

Hammering and hammering, sanding and scraping, rubbing & rubbing & rubbing, the grain lightening by the minute (*pale yellow, straw*) till the older layers start to come through.

188

Seesaw, Margery Daw
She saw seashells
down by the seashore

Forward & backward
Backward & forward
& upside-down-and-backward

like a hurdy-gurdy grinding

One-a-penny
Two-a-penny

Cranking it up
Giving it a spin

Clickety-clack
clickety-clack
Over & over
the same track

A rhyme in the wheels
A tune hung in the wires
                1
                5
                4

Gray
Yellow
Pink

like a handful of bobbing balloons

If you haven't any daughters
you can give them to your sons

5
4
3
2

One-a-penny
Two-a-penny
Hot cross buns

In and out, back and forth, tossing and turning and sighing like a diaphragm.

I feel sick. Seasick. This voyage in the clouds. Caravan, caravel. Pink and red shreds. Like flags planted, banners traveling . . .

Topmast
Topsail

Lines creaking
Wind strapped to the canvas
The canvas filling.

Then a clatter in the rafters. Ropes and tackle. Trying to tie things down . . . *I* know, *I* know,

Topmast
Topsail
Big Top

Cirrus

Every story happens somewhere.
"The sky is pale pink and pale yellow and pale gray. But Molly cannot sleep. It is *CIRCUS TIME.*"

Tap tap tap

Across the miles, from the far end of town . . .

> They're stretching the canvas
> to fit the frame
> Pounding down the pins

"Already the circus is unloading. And it is getting hotter."

No one else in the house was stirring. Not a peep not a mouse.

It is very early . . . It was once upon a time. . . . The day the circus came to town. The first book I could read.

Gray, yellow, pink, through a glaze of organdy. The curtain melting at her window. Sucking a little on the breeze. In & out. *Slip slap.*

> Elephants with switching tails
>
> Men with pails
>
> *Slip slop*
> goes the soapy tide
> inside
>
> Then *splish splash*
> over the gray hide
> that's tall as a tank
>
> *Skintight*
> *Bareback*
>
> *A bit*
> *of tin*
> *winking*
>
> *Yellow*
> *Pink*

"The house is very still.

"Tap tap tap. Someone is knocking at Molly's door. It is her Daddy. 'Good,' he whispers. 'You are ready. And now it's time to go.' "

Gray
Yellow
Pink

Lighter & lighter
Like blowing up a balloon

Her eyes getting bigger

Rap rap
Ratatat tat
The drumhead tightening

Hush go the brushes
over the drumskin
Pitter patter
Playing scat

"Molly takes her Daddy's hand. They are excited and they whisper together."

High wire
Tiptoe
What a balancing act

How they stand at the sill

one step away
from the sky

Gray
Blue
Blue with a greenish hue

His striped vision
scrolling the horizon
The whites of his eyes
flecked with birds
Fly from them they follow
Follow them they fly

Farther & farther
as the wedge widens

then narrows

Shrinks to a
pinpoint
Iris
Pupil

The two of them
dwindling

Molecule for
molecule
Air soft as
water

The dust from their tracks
dyeing the atmosphere
pink

Stains
Strains

Faint
Fainter

Their trail unwinding
down to the last
strand of DNA

Dot-dot-dash
Staccato
Pins & needles

A gap

blank as the ocean

Tap tap tap

Who cares
Too tired

Air
Water

It takes a fucking
acrobat to find
the line

Floor Plan

There were double windows behind the twin beds and down along the left wall in the room on Darby Road. There was a skylight window beside the tall bookcase in the recess above the closet that opened and closed using a long wooden pole with a metal crowbar attachment at the end. The walls were blue. There was wallpaper on the ceiling—a thicket of green and blue flowers sprouting from twisted twigs. Leaves and branches filled every window, sighing and chafing at night. First the tree frogs started up then the crickets, bringing the outside in.

On the other side of the wall Clare turned in her sleep. The headboard thumped.

The top stair creaked.

He was just looking for someplace he could get comfortable. He usually started out the night in their bedroom then moved to his study when Mother switched off the reading lamp on her bedside table after a couple of hours and it woke him. He might get in another hour down there.

She finally managed to drift off around three or four in the morning with the book in her lap, glasses slipped down the bridge of her nose. He came back up to find her that way, snoring, her lamp still burning, something on his mind.

She sat up. She felt the back of her head for her hairpins. Lifted the book in front of her face.

Other times she tried pretending to stay asleep.

She lowered the book, looked over the top, blinked behind her glasses, shrugged, put the book down completely, removed the glasses, yawned and wiped the moisture from the corners of her eyes.

What?

He went down to the kitchen to make himself tea.

The linoleum was cold on his bare feet.

He looked in her cupboards, opening every damn door and slamming it closed while he let the tea bag steep. Not a damn thing, not even a soda biscuit to take back down to the study with him.

In Europe he was up for hours before the rest of us. Brushed and dressed. He went out to get a copy of *The Herald Tribune* for Mother. Had a long conversation with the *propriétaire*, she made him tea.

First he kissed Clare good morning, then me. *Qu'avez-vous, Mademoiselle?* "Your breath is really bad, darling," he said. "You can do something about that."

He sat in the swivel chair at his desk, making a list for tomorrow. So many things to remember.

He took the afghan from his cot and tried stretching out on the other couch in the family room, beside the sliding glass doors. The plastic stuck to his cheek. A chill came in from under the drape. The birds started up an hour before dawn. Then every damn dog in the neighborhood. He may have dropped off for a bit somewhere around there.

He jerked awake, thinking he'd missed a step. The sky was pink. He just did make it down the hall to his bathroom.

Might as well go out and get the paper from the end of the driveway, there's no one up at this hour. Nothing they haven't seen before anyway.

That was the one luxury she allowed herself, toast and coffee and the newspaper in bed in the mornings on a tray. She left it to him to get the three of us up and on our way.

He mixed a pitcher of orange juice. In Iowa he used real oranges and an orange juice squeezer, he called himself the Barefoot Orange Juice Maker. The school bus was due at seven-fifteen. He came up the attic stairs to wake us.

She must have been dead to the world at that hour, way far away in another part of the house. Asleep finally.

She usually managed to drop off around five or six. First light. She put the book on the bedside table, her glasses beside it. Switched off the lamp. Her hands rested loosely in her lap. He claimed she snored.

He shifted his weight in the doorway.

Scratched his head.

Trying to remember.

Something about the Peloponnesian Wars maybe.

He held out his fingernails and sniffed.

That little bit of dandruff he couldn't seem to get rid of no matter what product he tried.

His other hand was on his side where the old incision still ached after all these years.

So much to take care of.

A hemorrhoid's a little piece of tissue that belongs on the inside but gets pushed out from having to spend so much time down in his bathroom. The best thing to do is just to take your finger and poke it back in.

Move over.

He lifted the covers, making room for himself in the narrow bed. He could still get in five or ten minutes before he had to go next door to wake Clare.

I tried pretending to be asleep.

In Europe I started getting up earlier so I could brush my teeth. I held my smile up to him.

Way back. Way far away. A long, long time ago, he put his hand there.

She shrugged her shoulders, she raised her hackles, she lifted the newspaper up to her face.

Lowered it, looked over the top, yawned.

What?

She sent him down to wake us.

How many times? How many times do I have to say it? *Slow obedience is no obedience.*

Observation and common sense.

You don't see what's right in front of your face.

Blue-green blossoms sprouting from twisting twigs.

You'll have to speak louder, she's on the other phone, it's his old phone down in the study, there's something wrong with it, she should take it back really, she's only renting the instrument, the phone company explained the whole thing to her, it's too complicated really, not worth the trouble, she can't afford it, you drive all the way out there and there's never a parking space, it's better if you just try to speak up.

Pencil, paper, busy signal.

He used to follow her from room to room, talking. He was at her heels, literally. She finally sank to the floor, she had to pretend to faint. Remember? What else could she do?

The room, the hall, the door, the house. Which goes where. What into what.

End, beginning, middle.

Some things it's better not to know, what good would it have done, it was better not to cross him, not to cross his path, don't even go down there.

We don't have to know about everything that happens, you can talk about other things, put some other words there, things are the way you say they are, put the rest of it out of your mind somewhere, in another part of the house.

Because I was afraid, Mother, I'm afraid to tell you, afraid you'll collapse on the stairs, moaning, your eyes rolling up into their sockets, your head will snap back, you'll say how much he loved me, how he loved all three of us, you'll say it wasn't true, Mother, I thought you didn't really want to know.

Besides you were far away, down at the opposite end of the hall, your door was closed, your hearing was going even then, you had to find some way to shut him out after all, what else could you do?

And it was so dark, wasn't it dark back then? It was dark behind your eyes, you didn't hear the stair creak did you, tell me, put some words in place of the darkness, put some other words there, talk to me, tell me another story about the way it was, a different story— Mother, make some more things happen with your words.

Once upon a time a long, long time ago, everyone was fine.

He couldn't have known anyway, he loved us, he couldn't have understood, could he, they don't know what they're doing when they do something like that, they're not in their right minds, he couldn't help himself, he put it away somewhere in a separate place, remember the poetry and the music, when we were in trouble he was the one we came to, he took care of us, when we were sick he drove us to the doctor, no one else could, when I stumbled he was the one who taught me how to walk all over again.

Black or white, salt and pepper, in his mind or out.

Middle, end, beginning, I don't know, I kept my eyes shut the whole time, some things go way way way way back, but they're never over.

A door a day, a dollar a scholar.

Even children have to have a job.

But I was still tired, I was always so tired, it was the same thing again and again.

He rubbed and rubbed.

I held still.

I was your good girl, Mother, I didn't squirm or make a fuss, I wouldn't give in, I thought about how it would be over, the way your mother taught you, I gripped the mattress, I looked at the picture of the man on the wall, all of Western literature pouring from his mouth, I relaxed my hands and let them lie by my sides with the palms turned out like Jesus.

He who understands all forgives all.

He taught me, he showed me, he told me things, Mother, I showed him my poems and he corrected them, I helped with his translations, I was his listener, his student, his supplicant down there in the study, I thought I'd been chosen, *he who understands all*, a writer has to know things, Mother, bear things, the words grew thick and briared, tongue stumbling over the Southern landscape then reaching up to the branches, crossing and recrossing, writing and rewriting, tapping and tapping at my window, trying to tell me, I thought there was a story only I could climb, sentence by sentence, my eyes pricked out by briars, that one day I'd read it and understand, I'd write it.

I wanted to die, Mother, lying in that adolescent room with the skylight window and the leafy wallpaper, at night I listened to the chiming crickets and the tree frogs and imagined they were calling me, I thought the darkness wanted me.

I thought there had been a mistake in time, a terrible mistake, a father had fallen in love with his daughter, maybe time flowed backward as well as forward, like the oroborus, the past could happen in the present, the present foretell the past, I knew it had happened once with Oedipus, I remembered Abraham preparing Isaac for sacrifice on the high altar, I thought about Jesus, but I didn't know there were others, I didn't know this happened to other daughters, no one told me, no one stepped out from the dark suburban woods that surrounded us to say this must not be permitted, the only law I knew were the laws of language.

But sometimes, Mother, I thought it was Patrick, in the *Rik-tik-tik* of the cicadas, I heard something stirring, chafing, uneasy in its chains, I smelled the undertow, I felt its warm breath, I thought maybe Patrick had cut through the woods and come up the hill to watch our house.

Echoes

Tap tap
bang bang bang
Rainbows splitting off the tin
Echoing

Silver
Rose
Complex harmonies

The steel tuned higher & higher
Pounded & pounded
till the sky's so thin it's ringing

A brazen cymbal
shivering like tinsel

Scored
Excoriated
Rubbed & rubbed & rubbed

till it's worn smooth
A satin path shining through

Then *bang slap* the sky snaps back
like a screen door
The whole world's a neighborhood

Keep it down
Keep your voice down
Don't bring that up
Do you want the people in the house next door
Do you want everyone on the block

Hammering & hammering away all those years
The same thing over & over
Backward & forward &
upside-down and backward
Pound pound pound

Pipe down do you hear me
Am I going to have to come in there
& knock some heads together

Whatever you say ricochets
The sky's adamant
The sky records everything

You made me
You made me
I have become your instrument

Silver & gold & sounding brass
My tongue is the sword of an angel
I will spare no one

Rattle rattle rattletrap
My teeth are jumping
I'm running on my rims

I heard the crack of dawn
I remember everything

Banter flatter chit chat
Rik-tikki-tik
Stop the rhyming
Stop the rhyming, chiming world

Oh who will deliver me
from the body of this childhood

Part 3

Wonderful Sound

They had him in the chair. His chin sagged on his chest. His tablet of paper and some books were on the table beside him but he made no move toward them. His left arm with the IV hung over the armrest so his fingers grazed the pole, his right hand lay limp in his lap. It was too much effort to lift his eyelids when I pushed the heavy door open.

My mother says it's the depression. There's no reason otherwise for him to get so downhearted, no new developments, physically speaking, just the same problems he's been having all along, his whole life really, a little worse now.

She tried getting him to talk to someone. A priest. Even a psychiatrist.

Remember that one fellow he was so fond of? He came over with the others during the War, Victor took poems to their sessions, too bad he's dead now.

The hospital chaplain couldn't get anywhere—not Episcopalian, of course, but with a degree, some very reputable place, Union Theological maybe.

Father Tom stops by yes but he has so many people to see, it's not his main job, hospital visitation, he uses the new man, she says, you know that nice young one they have now who assists at Communion, in his thirties, he always makes a point of greeting everyone young and old after the service, he's so outgoing, Victor's never liked him.

His left fingers twitched.

"Wendy," he said when I kissed his cheek, but his eyes stayed studying the floor. I hadn't seen him in over a month.

I put my purse down beside the chair. It was in his way if he wanted to get up and move around, but he didn't say anything. I picked it back up and put it on the window ledge on the part of the radiator where it wouldn't block the grate. I sat on the edge of the bed.

Were there errands he might need for me to run, supplies he'd forgotten to bring from home when he packed his bag or his student did—was it Eric? Was Eric back from his year abroad? Did he still come over sometimes for drinks?

This room's much more convenient than the last one, the nurses' station nearby and the elevator—I could take it down to the gift shop and be back in ten minutes.

He made a low noise in his throat after some things, giving the signal for agreeing to listen to someone, but that was all he could manage.

I sat with my hands in my lap, staring out the window. He sighed. Later he raised his head. He looked around the room.

"Now everything's clear," he said. His gaze traveled over the objects, his eyes looked washed.

But then a shadow passed—a curtain drawn back across. Something.

He said, "Now it's all confused. I'm all confused again." He let his eyes drift back to the floor. Hung his head.

There was a missing piece. My mother agreed. After supper she found the list, and I set up by the phone with pad and pencil.

Gastroenterologist, endocrinologist. Daddy had all the home numbers. His doctors didn't mind, he always said, they enjoyed his conversation, office visits left so little time.

Tonight each one was courteous, even gallant—*so this was Victor's daughter*—with the silvery manners my mother finds so soothing in Southern doctors.

Bloch, his original internist, home on a break from retirement in

Florida, said the body starts to give out at some point in time, Victor was an old man, we should be prepared given his age and history for things to begin to happen. Certain inevitable psychological accompaniments. Nothing anyone can do.

I put down the phone, and it rang. It was Clare's friend Mike. He thought he'd seen me at the hospital that afternoon from down the hall—really he thought I was Clare. So he called Patient Information and found out Victor had checked in.

He listened to my story and asked for it again. Yes, something was going on. He wanted to make a few calls. He said to tell Lillian even an Episcopalian is at the mercy of chemistry.

After I dropped her at her office, I spent most of the next morning in the corridors while my father had the transfusion Mike had talked Dr. Barbour into ordering. By the time they sent me up to his new room on Nephrology, it was time for his lunch to be delivered. I brought in his briefcase that had been left off the cart when they transferred his things.

He stood by the sink, rubbing at a spot on the washstand mirror. He wore a fresh gown and a pair of his undershorts from home.

A sideways look, then he addressed my reflection. He'd rolled the IV pole all the way over by himself: he was going to shave. The orderly promised to help him with a shower later.

He raised his left arm and flicked the cumbersome tube. At least they leave the patient the use of his good hand, the dominant one. A nuisance, but he'd manage.

His eyes in the mirror were like sparkling water.

I got the memo pad from the drawer and sat in the chair, writing down instructions as he gave them. Toothpaste, that new kind with baking soda if they carry it, he said, you might have to try his regular drugstore on Cornwallis, go right to the pharmacy in back and ask for his friend John Davies, he enjoys helping out. He'd probably appreciate hearing how my father's doing anyway.

The manila envelope with his notes for the Hagelstange translations inside, probably where he left it on the typing table in his study. He should be able to make some significant progress on the Hagelstange as long as they're keeping him here for a few days of observation, especially if someone's there to help him.

While he talked, he examined his face in the mirror in careful preparation for the act of shaving. Cheek, nose, cheek, chin—reclaiming the parts of himself in the light of the new day. He opened the cabinet mirror. Someone, probably one of those orderlies who still cares about doing his job, had taken the thought and effort to bring up his supplies from the old room and stock them on the new shelves. Daddy took down the necessary toilet articles—razor, shaving cream, a packet of blades, aftershave lotion—all brought with him from his own crowded medicine cabinet, his private bathroom off the study, his mornings at home.

Only a little awkwardly he lathered his face and made a quick test of the blade against his cheek. It would do.

He stepped back—considering. Sighed. Pure oxygen.

He spoke again to my image.

"At least you know now what your own death will be like."

Then he began from the back of the jaw forward to sweep through the lather with long strokes, his eyes wide and serious all the while, taking in the restored prospect of his face.

That evening he had me call Uncle Frank to report on things. A neighbor answered. She gave me a number for Patient Information at Chicago's Park Memorial, and the Operator put us through to the room. The brothers spoke hospital bed to hospital bed.

Frank said don't be alarmed. His doctor had him checked in so he could be seen by the top liver specialist. Remember how they'd suspected something? Well, now they knew. The liver man thinks this new medication just might do the trick, it was good news.

He remembered Dad's story about the doctor who tells his patient, "You know that thing you had before? Well, you've got it again." Then Daddy told the one about the doctor who records in his journal his own last words while taking his pulse. "Stopped."

It was two years later, after the last funeral, that Hadley told me how her father had steeled himself to get through the call. He gripped his hair by the roots to keep his head upright off the pillow and his voice steady the whole time they spoke.

He needed to get back the feel of being behind the wheel again. After all, if he got into trouble, I was right there next to him. And it was only what, six, maybe seven miles? His first time in the car since he'd been home from the hospital, his first outing—if you could call it that.

We pulled into a space on the paved half of the parking lot. On the gravel part, a back hoe and a steamroller sat vacant and motionless. He groaned. You'd think if they have the wherewithal to put up a whole complex of new clinics and install their so-called state-of-the-art equipment, they could finish a simple parking lot on time. "State of the art"—another colorless euphemism for something we already knew how to say. Wasted language.

He turned over his records to the nurse at the reception desk. Naturally she got it wrong and asked what time was he scheduled for treatment. He told her we were only there for the tour.

We followed her down the hall from the reception area to a large room at the back of the building. It was fitted out for patients: row after row of recliners, like chaise longues, each with a folding chair and small magazine table beside it. There was medical equipment at every station, monitors and dials intimidating as the rows of choices inside a voting booth. It all sat idle though, like the craning machinery in the parking lot, except for one person hooked up at the far end.

The nurse-receptionist motioned us in that direction, insisting on introductions.

The girl was flipping through *Seventeen* with her free hand. She looked about seventeen.

She obliged the nurse with a brief account of the miracle of her own dialysis. Back in school now. Almost caught up with her class.

We didn't ask questions, and she returned to the full-page spread on versions of the new Princess Di cut.

Back in her office, the nurse went into detail. It was a fairly recent development that such an advanced technology was being made available to the general public in an outpatient setting, the idea being that a patient can accommodate visits to the clinic to his or her own schedule where the procedure becomes part of a normal routine.

She told my father what to expect in his relationship with the new technology.

He would need to come in three times a week, his time on the machine would be approximately three hours. Afterward, maybe for most of the next day, he'd feel a little weak, even nauseated. But by the second day—well, it wouldn't quite work out that way during the week what with his timetable being every other day, but he could certainly enjoy a day or two of feeling like his old self by the weekend.

There was one alternative. It inspired her to lean forward over her crossed arms, elbows on the desk. There were variations of the prototype that could travel. In-home machines. The patient could learn to perform the procedure for himself in the comfort of familiar surroundings—with, of course, the help of a caring partner.

In the parking lot he handed over the keys to me without explanation. He didn't say anything for some time except to mention when he ran his finger over the dashboard how dirty my mother let her side get.

After I made the left at the 7-Eleven and then right at the corner and through the Valley gates, he said none of his daughters had ever mastered proper timing in the use of the turning signal.

Good days, bad days. He already had bad days. He felt nauseated *now*, he felt weak. What if his good day off from dialysis turned out to be one of his bad days? He couldn't sit with those people anyway day after day in those chairs. What would he say to them? What did they have in common? Not to mention the nurses and technicians fussing around him, having to listen to their inanities. It wasn't the kind of setting he'd ever felt comfortable in. His was a solitary nature. The poet's always is.

He said imagine Lillian trying to help him cleanse his blood. Operating a delicate machine like that. Operating *any* machine.

He'll go back to the hospital and have them implant the shunt in his arm. When things start to get bad again, he can check himself in for another transfusion. Hadn't the doctors said the electrolyte imbalance might remain stable for as long as six months initially?

In the driveway he had the old trouble with the passenger side seat belt, but he batted away my help. Lillian had the damn thing in such a tangle. As usual. He said just sit there while he got it straightened out. He needed to rest a minute anyway.

After another minute he said, "You do know don't you this is what will get me in the end?"

She can't help it. When he drifts across the divider, she braces herself. He accuses her of bad faith. His own wife won't trust him with her life.

He quotes Frederick the Great rousing his troops to the battlefront. "Dogs! Would you live forever?"

It makes her so nervous, but what choice does she have? He's turned down all offers from her secretaries, people at Church. He says she wants to give away the keys to his kingdom before he's even started the journey to Saint Peter's gate.

Has he failed her up to now? Has he faltered in his traces? Does she think a little fluctuation in blood chemistry would keep him from his appointed rounds? Get her to the office by nine, take the cleaning tickets to the cleaners, execute the orders on her shopping list. She's been satisfied with the service she's gotten through forty years of marriage—suddenly she wants to fire the chauffeur?

He insists on making the dark drive out to the airport whenever any of us flies in to stay with him. Why call a cab when we can still get *him* for free? If it makes Lillian jumpy, let her stay home, it's not as if she's ever been good company. If he did have some kind of emergency on the road, she'd hardly be in a position to take over behind the wheel would she. He knows the route. Her program would have gone bust years ago if he hadn't provided the shuttle service from airport to campus for all her friends. He can do it with his eyes closed.

But it's the same with her daughters. Another nagging female when he pulls into the floodlit parking area outside Baggage Claim.

He must be tired from the long trip out there at the end of his day, I say, why not let me drive, I never get to drive since I moved to the city, I miss the feel of it, it would give me pleasure.

I hold my breath through the weaving black miles of Interstate, clutching the armrest on my mother's side.

He switches lanes, right to left, and a car set to pass us honks furiously from behind.

"I've been signaling for over fifty years—let *them* figure it out for a change," he says.

Back to the right lane, up against the towering wall of a semi. He starts to make his move again, pulls back, starts. Margaret's lucky her fear of flying forces her to take the bus or her own car when it's her turn to stay with him.

He dreams of catching the drops on his tongue. An orange so ripe the juice oozes from the rind. He craves freshness. His body demands it. None of the supplements the doctors have prescribed—calcium tablets, high dosages of vitamin C—can appease the longing for moisture and starch deep in his cells.

She's starving him besides. Look how the ribs are beginning to show. Those thawed out dinners she comes home to prepare. Frozen vegetables, frozen fish. Low sodium doesn't mean a thing when you've immobilized the nutrients like that.

If she comes home at all. If she's even in town and not off God-knows-where at some conference, some invented obligation.

Daughters are no substitute for a proper wife, no matter how much he enjoys our visits. It's her fault we never learned our way around a kitchen, well Margaret, she had to master a few menus when she got married the first time.

Thank God he's not too weak yet to sit through dinner at a restaurant.

He has cases of bottled water delivered weekly, ordered from that special place his student told him about. Sometimes he goes out and stands at the end of the driveway to wait so the driver won't miss the house. They have interesting conversations.

When there's a break in his routine as Lillian's errand boy, he drives all the way across town to the new vegetable market. It's by the railroad tracks near the old mill, two blocks from that convenience store where he used to pick up the *Times* for her on Sunday—he can still find his way.

Colors piled beside the sidewalk. Heaping stacks of lemons, limes, juice oranges, and the other kinds. Like something you'd see in a real city—the owners moved here from up North.

White grapefruit, pink grapefruit, all varieties of apples, even Cortlands—he'd thought they just didn't grow them anymore. Bins of lettuce, Boston, romaine, Bibb. Watercress and garden cress—the woman showed him how to distinguish them. Leeks. No other source in nature for those vitamins, whatever they are. He thinks he can remember how his grandmother prepared them if Lillian will pay attention to his directions.

There's a sign over the awning: ORGANICALLY GROWN.

We never had that down here before.

People in the South don't know about vegetables, how to cook them properly, there's probably an historic explanation. Privation during the Civil War. They treat vegetables like meat—something you have to kill first. Cooked till they're dead and flat, all the taste boiled out, like something served at a school cafeteria. Or his own dinner table. When it doesn't come from a package.

The woman wants to talk about his feelings. He could swear the word comes up in every third sentence that exits her mouth. It has no meaning. Words lose their effectiveness when you toss them off indiscriminately that way.

How he let Lillian talk him into these visits in the first place he can't imagine. If she thinks he's gotten so incompetent he needs a babysitter, she should quit her job and stay home. So what if it means they'd starve, he's starving now.

Feelings aren't something you can assault with the intellect.

Does this woman think he'd have let her into the house in the first place, if he wasn't feeling rotten?

He has more to say to the maid than he does to someone with her kind of bland, social worker mentality.

She has a strange smell—not a pleasant one either. He finally had to bring it up with her directly, he was sorry to but he really had no choice. She didn't seem offended, actually. She told him the name of her perfume and went on with whatever it was they were discussing at the time.

Feelings, probably.

Well, what does she care if he has to spend the hour after she leaves gagging into his toilet?

Hospice, from the Latin *hospitium,* hospitality, the stem *hospes,* host, receiver of guests. Referring to a shelter for travelers or the destitute. Typical American approach, to turn the whole concept upside down. Making *him* the host—he's hardly up to it.

He had her read a little of the Kleist to him the other morning. As long as she's there, he has to find things for her to do.

Next week he might get her started on *The Man Without Qualities.* Give it a proper reading, front to back, he never had the time for it while he was teaching.

She has no languages, of course. He tried to explain to her some of the problems involved in translation. How it takes years of practice to find the pulse of one language in the syntax of another. He doubts she understood, but she seemed interested.

She has a few small problems of her own that have profited by his advice. She'd never heard of his technique of sucking on a lemon to control nausea.

She takes over at the wheel now and then on their trips across town to make his purchases at the vegetable stand. She taps the melons and listens to the sound. She knows how to choose an avocado by testing the tip—she has a feel for it.

One weekend when I arrive in a taxi from the airport, he greets me at the kitchen door dressed for the cocktail hour in his suit and slippers. The glasses are lined on the counter beside the ice tray and a bowl of peanuts. There's a full quart of bourbon and even a bottle of Dubonnet for me. He points with shining eyes.

"Mrs. Murray and I went to the liquor store today." He boasts, "She let me drive, coming back."

"Give me those!"

He snatches the set of keys from my hand.

His bark echoes against the concrete walls of the hospital garage.

It's hard to anticipate. Sometimes he heads straight for the passenger side and slumps down in the seat with his eyes closed. Not a word the whole way home.

Other days the mere effort required to open the car door is beyond him. He stands mutely beside it. Is it too much to expect the other person to notice? To read the signals of a man in distress?

Some kind of delaying action's best. A hesitation step as you approach the vicinity of the Buick. Fish for something in your purse, scan the sky for weather.

We know by now how to take the tempo from him—his moods, his bodily aches. How his frailty can snap.

"Let go! Let go of my elbow!" One leg over the chain barrier that cordons off the grassy triangle from the sidewalk—a shortcut to the outpatient entrance.

"You treat me like some kind of invalid."

Then he totters, flails for my arm.

"Help! Help!"

Vexed by my neglect.

Would she mind helping her husband? He gets dizzy, bending down—she should know that by now.

She does know doesn't she how to put a man's socks on his feet?

He has to save energy. All this running around, it's a drain on the resources. He needs to conserve for the more important things. He could have written three, five articles this week alone in the time he's spent gallivanting all over town for her.

Pull them up straight the way he likes.

Now give him room to breathe.

He'll manage.

He *said* he can manage.

Relax, dammit. Go rearrange the pins in her hair. She's not due at her office for another fifteen minutes, and he can make it door to door in twelve.

He's resting. Has she never seen a man rest before?

No. Don't. Don't wake her. Let her sleep away the morning. Why else would she come home for a visit?

She's no driver anyway. He wouldn't put his car at risk. An automatic requires a different touch than that clumsy straight shift on her battered VW.

If he's not up to his manly duties this once, Lillian can call the neighbors. Their car's there all day, that woman has nothing to do.

West-something. Weston. It's on the mailbox for anyone with eyes.

The rocker creaks.

He has to grip the arms and lower his head to push himself forward into a standing position.

He gags.

"Get away! Get away!"

Gags again. Then groans back into the chair.

"Have you no mercy, woman?"

Bring him the book. *He'll* call them.

The phone book! Beside the phone!

Why are her hands trembling?

Are you the driver?

If you're so smart you think you know what to do, I'll get out of the car and we'll change places, and you sit in the driver's seat, you see how it feels.

Never raise your voice to a person who's driving.

216

I've been behind the wheel for six decades, I should know what I'm doing by now.

My entire afternoon was wasted on your chores, you'd think I could expect a little friendly conversation on the ride home, an attentive audience.

I must have driven a hundred miles today. All from point A to point B. Stuck behind a school bus the whole way. Stop and start. Start and stop. The man used his brakes like a maniac.
None of you would have the patience. The judgment.

Certain faculties underdeveloped in the female, a side of the brain.

Watch it! Watch it! Watch it!

Maybe you can find yourself another husband, but try finding yourself a driver.

I can still drive, can't I? I can still get you to the Church on time.

If Wendy's the one doing the driving, I'd rather stay home and die. She didn't miss a single pothole last time, I was counting.

Ouch!
I said: Ouch!
I'd like to make it to the Emergency Room in one piece, if you could try.

One of you girls will have to take your mother there and pick her up afterward. I can't manage this family from a hospital bed.

At least I'll be dead. I'd rather be dead than on the road once your mother's been licensed to kill.

Let the Driver's Training driver drive her there. She's paying for his time. That's more than I ever got.

He said a few hours away from the hospital might do me some good. Just drive me around the campus. I have to be back by three.

Around the block a few times, I guess. I haven't been home in so long. Just up to the Church and back.

That's fine. That's enough. We'd better go home so I can pack the rest of my things.
Everything looks so beautiful.

The woman was redistributing the flowers in the vase beside his bed. Not Mrs. Murray but the one they sent to replace her when Mrs. Murray told the hospice people she wouldn't be coming to see him any longer. Some personal situation—she couldn't give details.

This new woman didn't look up to see who'd come in. She gestured toward my father with her head as if it were an extra arm she could employ while her other ones were occupied.

"I think he's trying to say something."

She stood by while I went over and bent to the moving lips.

There was a string of words, then a word by itself, repeated. He was half in and half out of it, talking or listening to something, then trying to reach back to us with whatever it was.

"What does he want?" The volunteer woman moved in. She might need the information for some report.

Her questions seemed to agitate him further, and he worked over the words until a light saliva foamed from between his dry lips.

"Vuh, vuh," he said, and "guh."

I nodded. "Yes." I smoothed his head. I spoke over my shoulder. "Something," I told the woman, who wouldn't leave us alone. "It's about God, I think."

"Say what?"

"God. He said, 'Voice of God.'"

Tears started down the old man's cheeks. He tried for more.

"I can feel Him," he whispered in my ear. "Walking around."

His throat struggled to deliver it.

"Tremendous power."
He wept and wept.

By nightfall he was back. Mother came after work, and the three of us drank sherry from the mini bottles I'd saved from my flight.

He was sitting in a chair in a clean gown, his hand without the IV holding the paper cup. He brought it to his mouth and back down now and then without drinking, satisfied with the ceremony. He was quiet—all three of us were. Letting the room sounds take over. A ticking. A hum. Beneath the surface, his new blood ran along the old paths.

I spoke up. "There're some people down the hall from West Virginia."

He nodded: his part.

"I bet they're taking swigs from a bottle right now," I said.

It was the kind of story he liked.

"It's probably white lightning."

He raised his own drink and looked at it. Wet his lips with his tongue.

"Wonderful phrase," he said, *"white lightning."*

Frank died in July. Daddy took the call in his study—he was home again. He took down from the shelf the oversized journal he was using for that year, and wrote:

> My brother, Frank, died this morning. 10:15 A.M.,
> Memorial Hospital, Highland Park, Ill., age 78 years,
> 64 days. Peace to his soul!

The fluctuating chemicals in his bloodstream had made his handwriting shaky for months now.

He wouldn't talk about it. It was all in his eyes—wide and accusing.

We sat for an ordinary dinner. I had to drive Mother to the airport the next morning for some weekend conference in Atlanta.

Daddy was sunk in his chair, the table at eye level, as if he'd lost all the height added to him since he was a boy. When he started to cry it was like a child too—his features dissolving into grief without transition.

"What is it?" Mother asked, her vocal chords tightening. "Is it Frank?"

Something like a nod from Daddy's chair.

"Oh. Oh, now. Do you think he would have wanted you to go on about it this way?"

Another time she said: "Would you have wanted him to keep living with the kind of pain he was in?"

Frank wasn't a believer. There was no funeral. A small group of neighbors and friends gathered at the house out in the garden Frank planted every spring since his retirement. He grew vegetables for their table, early and late flowers from the terra-cotta pots and bowls Harriet brought home from her class. He walked his grandson, Kate's first child, around the little fishpond he'd designed and answered his questions about the universe. Every fall before they shut down the house to go to Mexico, Frank covered the flower beds with wood chips.

Daddy didn't attend the simple ceremony. He wasn't expected to travel in his condition.

He didn't ask about the ashes, the horror was too great.

They'd argued about it. Those letters back and forth every week, phone conversations, visits. When Uncle Frank came to see us, we took him to Church, where he sat in the pew in his scratchy shirt and no tie where everyone could see, watching his brother assist at the Eucharist, silver haired and distinguished in the black cassock and white cotta.

But Frank stayed unregenerate. He refused to hope.

It frustrated Daddy.

Frank should have been like him—scholar, translator, poet. He could have been. He wouldn't.

It did no good to write those letters home to Dad about all the drinking going on in their rooms in Princeton. No use when Victor begged Frank to leave the bars and come back to the hotel that summer the young men traveled together through France and Spain. Why did Frank waste himself? Why did he go into business? Victor wanted to keep them together—even into heaven—the way they were as boys. But Frank was always just beyond his younger brother's reach, 595 days ahead of him, always teasing.

While Victor got his festschrift in North Carolina, Frank was volunteering for the adult education program at a local college outside Chicago. Every Wednesday night, in his rumpled retirement clothes and Hemingway beard, he taught a course he called the History of the World Backward.

His own world. He was his own man.

Dust now. As if he'd never happened.

All that time the two of them lived through—over half the modern age—who could vouch for it now that Frank's body had gone up in smoke? Victor was alone with his childhood for the first time.

Better to let the worms have you. Grow like a tuber, interlocking with the rest of the root system. Better to live underground. Wife and daughters, the generations after to visit his grave and remember. He couldn't be taken away entirely if there was a place on the earth that still said the name Victor.

He looked for the Resurrection of the Dead and the Life Everlasting. The Christian promise. Every prayer and poem, his years of service in the Church were offered in that hope—that Jesus would come one day and find him and restore him. He must wait for Him. He must keep his body in wait. *This* body. Wasn't that the promise? The same body restored to the believer—intestines, bowels, everything repaired and renewed? He needed one more chance with this body to find the love of the woman who could understand him.

He lowers his head between his knees, swallows deeply, and expels the air. Swallows again. The same thing over again until he can raise the long roll of belches that relieves the nausea.

He has on boxer shorts and a T-shirt—he's gotten that far. The socks he's brought down to the family room with him. He'll show me how. He can help. If he leans back in the captain's chair and pushes while I pull, it's not that difficult an operation.

He wants to be finished with everything by the time Lillian's secretary brings her home. He'll surprise her. Then she'll say how nice he looks all dressed up in his clothes.

It works out when his day goes according to schedule. After her morning ride comes for her, he takes a nap to make up for the sleep he missed the previous night—it gives him that little reservoir of energy he needs to get his day started, then he draws his first bath.

It's easier now with one of the three of us home so frequently. Mrs. Murray made such mistakes, she never learned where things were kept. And he doesn't have the time now, with so few weeks between hospital stays, to teach someone everything from the ground up.

The bath water should be very hot, otherwise it won't do a thing for the hemorrhoids. But it leaves him feeling terribly weak afterward. He recuperates on the cot in his study, listening to the *Noon Hour* on Public Radio. Their news stories are so much more complete. Most people don't take the time it requires to become fully informed, they just have opinions.

Then *Classical Afternoon* featuring a different composer every week.

He has the volume turned up so we can listen from the family room when I bring down lunch on a tray.

So much light streaming through the glass doors he's not even chilly like this, in his skivvies.

Bad Ischl, where Brahms probably wrote this trio, was the Emperor's summer residence in the Austrian Salzkammergut.

He gives me back his plate. He finished the whole sandwich!

There's an apple in the bottom part of the refrigerator. You know. The vegetable bin. Bring it down with the paring knife. If it's not in the silverware drawer, try the dishwasher—everything's clean. He remembered to turn it on this morning, but someone else will have to be in charge of unloading it.

He halves the apple and quarters it. Halves the quarters. Scoops a shallow boat in each to remove the seeds. Uses the saucer he sent me back to the kitchen to get for the discards.

Each step requires concentration, his reserves are dwindling. He's always been meticulous.

He bets I never even take the trouble of cutting up an apple for my lunch. None of us. No matter how often he's gone over the proper method.

Fruit's so important to the diet.

He hands me a slice. When I've finished, he serves the second one.

How many times, how many years of minutes out of our lives has he slowed down and drawn to himself this way? His gestures, his every move. The sound of his breathing.

Watch now. Are you watching? Maybe you'll learn something.

A fly settles on his knee. A crumb he spots. Wait. Don't move, don't get up. He has to tend to it.

Years we'll never get back.

Minutes that go on forever.

A sudden emergency hoists him from the chair. He heads out the door, swaying on old men's sea legs. Down the hall, his body pitched at a frantic, oblique angle.

But he doesn't make it. I follow the line of discrete turds—a path to his bathroom—picking up after him.

Don't say anything, he says. Please. Lillian's so sensitive.

There's still time if we hurry. He can take a second bath and then get his shave in.

It's Mother who's late, it turns out. He says, "The news started seven minutes ago," as he takes the glass of bourbon from her.

He's powdered and sweet with aftershave. He chose the smoking jacket, and I got the meerschaum from the rack in his study and the pouch of Turkish tobacco his student gave him in the hospital. All neatly laid out on the humidor beside his chair—though he probably won't smoke. He told the student when he thanked him, he doesn't enjoy it now the way he used to.

It wasn't long until bourbon turned on him too—first the taste, then he couldn't even stand to have the smell around him. Mother told the funeral visitors that was when she knew the end was near. They all laughed through their tears over the last days of Southern gentlemen.

He stumbles under the portrait, so I grab his elbow and lead him over to one of the dining room chairs to wait the weakness out.

Lillian had him sit for that painting when he was home for so many weeks after the first hospitalization all those years ago in the other house. The artist was that woman from Church. She's dead now, or else her husband is. Or they moved away.

God knows why he let Lillian talk him into it, he was on cortisone. The cheeks are all puffed out and he has that unnatural tan.

She wanted a matching pair for the one of her hanging in the front hall, his student did that portrait in Marshall. She doesn't look like herself. The mantilla, the olive tones—you can tell the boy was under some influence or other. She always says no wonder she looked so solemn, with a baby and two toddlers running around outside the frame.

He thinks he can make it now. I help him up, and he holds to the wall a minute, staring down at his bare feet, before starting on his path to the stairs and on down to his bathroom.

He says, "I hope you don't remember me this way."

He worries about us, especially me.

What will happen once he's no longer around? What is it I really want to do with my life?

"I want to be a great writer," I tell him.

He sighs. "That's the hardest thing of all."

Now they're ready for him. Now? At eleven-thirty in the morning?

If he has his bath now, he'll miss the lunch trays when they come around. Then he'll spend another long afternoon starving, without so much as a saltine in his stomach to absorb the medication properly.

Didn't they get his note? He specifically asked to be taken early, right after the boy came to give him his shave. He wrote out the instructions at the bottom of last night's menu and gave it to the girl to leave at the nurses' station.

Well, it doesn't surprise him. He thought there was something dull about her, she wouldn't look him in the eye.

Forget it. Do it their way then. Why consider the patient's needs when you're running a big, important hospital like this one.

Hospital, from the Latin *hospitalis*, of a guest.

He's going to need some help if he's expected to get into this contraption without injuring himself.

Wendy, he says, put down the book.

At least he has a daughter there who knows how to follow orders. Sometimes.

Take his arm and let the nurse—is it Miss or Mrs. Finn—stand there and hold the wheelchair steady. He'll signal when he's ready to lower himself.

Now. No! Not that way! Can't she see what she's doing? The metal thing just dug right into his ankle. If you push it at him like that, he'll trip and fall backward. Gently. Easy, easy. All right. Now. Let go.

Let go or you'll break his arm in two.

I take his book and my purse. His glasses in the purse. I follow in his train down the hall.

Too bad he can't use the bathtub in his own room. If that doctor, what's-his-name, Daily, had lanced the hemorrhoid properly in the first place, he wouldn't have to go to all this trouble using high technology.

Yes. He knows all about it. The red button for emergencies, the temperature dial. The other nurse—older, with the mole—explained everything the last time.

Just check the dial and then leave him to do his business.

Higher. This temperature won't do him any good. He needs it hot. Try raising it half a setting.

Now lower.

Just one notch.

Between the next two.

225

Forget it.

Just forget it.

Leave it where it is. So what if he comes out looking like a patient from the burn ward. At least he'll have had a few hours relief from the torment in his bottom.

She'll stay. Wendy, stay, he says. Would he have had me come all this way if he didn't need me in there? There're places he can't reach. They wouldn't have him in a hospital if he were capable of doing everything himself.

He needs the human contact besides. He spent the whole night last night alone.

She'll be fine, he tells the nurse, she brought a book. There's a chair there for the helper next to his tub. Wendy won't mind, she's used to heat, after all, his daughters are Southern girls.

If he thinks it's getting to me, he'll send me out for some air.

Go. He says, go. Leave us in peace. Make sure the door's shut tight.

Don't start there. Go back a paragraph or two so he can pick up the thread of the narrative.

He says you're losing interest, aren't you, he can tell by my tone. I'm not putting expression into my voice.

He'd rather talk anyway, he never gets the chance.

No one comes around.

Things on his mind.

That place. There. In the middle of his back. He'll hold the scrub brush, and I can reach over and guide him to the trouble spot.

He's worried about Lillian. She's working too hard. Back and forth to the hospital, in and out on her breaks. He barely has a chance to exchange a sentence with her.

They're having troubles, he thinks his daughters should know. She doesn't listen, she won't take his advice. There isn't that common ground they had when they were first married. She was so sweet back then, an innocent—the three of us would have been amazed.

The spot on his back is red and scaly from so much rubbing. Long scratches there too where he's tried to get at the bone ache through T-shirts and pajama tops with a pen or pencil or his dinner fork. We gather the bloody laundry and do it at home.

He signals he's ready. One hand on the side of the tub to steady himself, the other arm given over. It's unmuscled as a preadolescent boy's. His face almost unlined. "Cornflower blue" is how Mother would remember his eyes.

Careful now. Careful. One leg at a time. Now the towel. He pats the gray bush under his stomach. Reaches back to his sore behind where the flesh hangs loose and wrinkled. I grasp his arm again, work it like a lever when he bends to rub down his spindly shanks.

He props one foot on the opposite knee, takes a corner of the towel, and works it between each toe. Then the reverse—he starts in and stops.

Lifts his blue gaze to ask, "Do you think your mother and I should get a divorce?"

She knew it would make him feel better just to hear her say the words. He was always after her, but she couldn't.

Something about her.

She couldn't profess to what she didn't feel in her heart.

Oh she stands by her Church. She always has. Bury her in Episcopal ground when her time comes. Those beautiful words from the Book of Common Prayer said over the coffin. A nice hymn.

"One Catholic and Apostolic Church, one Baptism for the remission of sins"—she made her catechism long ago when she was just a girl in Albany.

But she could never accept the idea of an afterlife. No matter how much Victor harangued her.

Maybe she and Frank were alike after all.

She thought he didn't want to talk about it, most people don't.

Then the next morning she'd find lines for one of those poems scribbled on the back of an envelope. "Eclipse." "The Death of the Rose."

A book he translated years ago left open on his night table, a passage underlined in pencil.

Leave your overcoat and hat.
Go as you are. Nothing you need down here
but your old blindness.

What could she have said though, really? What can anyone say about death?

But he tells us she won't even let him bring up the subject.

He's brought us all together one last time.

Or else he'll pull through.

They may be able to give him back to his family for a little while longer—he might still have a few weeks.

She couldn't take the chance though.

She hated disrupting our lives—Margaret with her new husband, Clare her important job and boyfriend, me at that writers' thing. She telephoned each of us with the same message: "The doctors say I should think about calling his daughters to the bedside."

He eats and we watch. He doesn't want conversation, complains if there is any. No commotion either. Just do what he asks when he asks it. Cut his meat for him, get a tissue from the box on the window ledge to wipe his chin. Sit still while he eats his meal. Sit with him.

Do we have something better to do?

Only the blunt sounds of his cutlery. His steady chewing. Eyes on his plate, his chin an inch above the food tray.

It's the chemical imbalance that drags him down, slowing the motions of the fork to his mouth and back again. His eyelids droop. Baleful looks. Heavy lidded silence.

The way it's always been. He's brought us all back.

Did we think they could wriggle out of it? Get off scot free? Did we hope to escape—Margaret to a better marriage, Clare to have children he'd never know?

Let this be a lesson then. A reminder. The deadly silence between the knock of utensils, the chink against the water glass. The unspoken accusation: we're the ones. We've done it. Ruined his meal, his evening, his day. Ended his life.

His three middle-aged daughters, his middle-aged wife. Gathered together. On the edge of our seats. Tense to interpret the slightest signal. Clare holding his glasses, in case he needs to see something. Me with my hands folded in my lap, proper, prayerful.

Let it be done. Get it over with. Let death come, let death be over.

The Church was running out of room. All the best sites were being bought up.

He found out from sorting through some papers she left out.

He said, "You put the money down for *two* of them?"

She was so nervous at having gone behind his back, she thought she might faint right there in the hall. The last thing she expected was his bursting into tears.

He said, "I was afraid. I wasn't sure you'd want to be buried next to me."

It got so her hands were shaking from the moment she heard him call to her.

Even at work, away from him, it would start at her typewriter. She worried she wouldn't be able to perform on the job.

When she got a clean T-shirt from his drawer, he found a hole in it. She brought him socks, but they were the wrong color.

You know how bad she always was about standing up to him.

She couldn't go on though.

"Whatever you tell me to do, you say I got it wrong."

He sat in the bedroom rocker, looking down.

He said, "I'm aware of that."

He stood with his coat buttoned up and his hat on. They were going out the kitchen door—it was the last time.

No, the last time was the ambulance. It must have been the one before.

Mike was waiting in the driveway with his car.

She had the suitcase *and* the briefcase—he was that weak.

She knew how to recognize the signs by then. When she told him he'd be better off where they could give professional care, he didn't even object. He was so sick he probably didn't care *where* he was.

She held open the screen, waiting to help him with the steps. She thought he'd stopped to rest.

He turned as if he were going back inside the house. Just stood there, looking around the room.

"I liked living here," he said. "It was nice."

The night before he'd knelt on the carpet next to her side of the bed, crying.

"I was such a nice little boy. If only you'd known me then."

I think he knew, she says, don't you? I think it was his way of expressing it when he said those things, maybe he really *was* sorry.

It was too late, though. The damage had been done.

He's in and out. They told her the most they can do now is make him comfortable.

Yesterday they came by on rounds, and he tried to grab one of them by the lapels.

"The truth!" he demanded. "Tell me the truth, Doctor."

He grappled with the white coat and the man struggled the other way.

Victor asked him, "Will I still be able to get an erection?"

Another time, he confessed, "I had about a drink and a half, then I turned myself in."

It's hard on her, doing it alone.

He must have heard the ring despite all the noise from outside his door. He was pointing and signaling, so she had to lift the phone from the bedside table and stretch the cord to put the receiver next to his ear.

He said, "Wendy." Then, "I'm really quite cheerful."

He comes and goes though, she can't say for sure. This might be it if you want to see him before it's over.

* * *

Monday would be better than Sunday, most people don't read the Saturday paper, they'll miss the announcement.

Easier on Father Tom too not to have to do two services in one day.

Of course, it all depends on when it happens.

She settles back, tucking her legs under her skirt, rubbing the arch of one foot over the instep of the other so the nylon makes that sound.

He might linger past the weekend.

No one knows, they can't tell her for certain, nothing's set in stone.

"*Ja, ja.*" Gerda's accent is rich with woe. She's been like family— so much back and forth to the hospital, that dangerous highway in the pitch dark—pass her the plate.

It's real Southern shortbread, someone from Church baked it, people have dropped off all kinds of food.

She has to raise her glasses above the bridge of her nose to wipe the fresh moisture from her eyes.

Callers morning and night, people telephoning, even at the office, she's afraid she won't get her work done.

Well, people need people, what's that line, the comfort of strangers, that's all anyone has in the end, the doctors and nurses, sometimes the last person to hold your hand is the hand of a stranger.

It's hard getting out of life. Her voice cracks. It's hard to *watch*.

Gerda was there. She saw, didn't she?

Ja, terrible. Terrible. Gerda nods and shakes her head. Her eyes shine—the dire whites. She warns me I won't even recognize Victor when I see him in the morning.

How can that be? What more can have happened to him?

He's always been himself, no matter how sick, he's still been Victor. What disease or medicine could go so far, to leave a different body in the bed?

Let them try. Let them do their worst. Swab the hospital corridors, scrub down the walls of his room—there's no disguise that can keep him from me, I'll find him in the least vestige.

As I always have.

231

Lilac vegetal, witch hazel, violet water. A step on the stair. In what extremity would I not know my own father?

You know how stiff those men are with each other at the beginning of a conference, she says, someone needs to be there the first night to get things started, check on the setups, dinner and the cocktail party, go over the schedule with them, one of my secretaries was ready to step in but now there's a sick baby involved.

You can get away long enough to drive me, there's nothing anyone can do for him anymore but sit there, I'll have the whole day on Sunday for that and tomorrow I'll bring my lunch over the way I always do.

A drop more—here—then, really, it's past midnight. Gerda never knows when to leave, rest is important just now, everyone says it's hardest on the family, people forget.

She says, "I enjoy being with you so much." She lowers the book so when I bend down to the bed she can reach my cheek. She says, "You're a good friend to the world."

They've raised the guardrails and strapped his wrists to them. When I first see him he's pulled himself over to one side, gripping the righthand bars so hard the tendons swell with the strain. He's trying to raise himself—or get out. He's whimpering, mouthing words to the empty room. Blood trickles from one nostril.

He's thin to the bone. When I reach around his torso, I can feel the cricket of his pulse scattering everywhere. His heat in my arms crackles from the static of so much contact with the pillow and sheets.

The words come out, "Help me, help me."

I untie his wrists, try to get him in the center of the bed. But his freed arms swim against the air, unsure of what they want, which direction.

"Help me," he repeats. His eyes dart—knowing there's someone, it doesn't matter who. "Hold my back."

When the nurses come in to change his sheets, they don't mention the loosened restraints—as long as there's a daughter there to watch him. They push the body first on one side then the other, rolling him like a log. He submits. He's a thing, a category, "dying old man," between their ministrations.

"Help me sign my name," he says. I find a pen in his bedside drawer and the tablet of paper and prop him in the circle of one arm and with my free hand over his guide his signature.

It's palsied but recognizable, the two of us working together.

His pain's everywhere. When I press him to me, bracing his whole frame as tight as I can, he still moans and cries out, "Hold me! Hold my back!" as if I weren't, as if I could go deeper to find where he's suffering so.

I stop his nurse in the corridor to ask about the dosage of painkiller he's getting. A Mrs. Tate. The woman consults the clipboard crooked in her arm.

She says, "It's not pain so much as restlessness."

"He's in constant pain."

"He hasn't said anything. He's never asked for more morphine."

We're toe to toe outside the door of an old man whose speech is reduced to moans and popping sounds.

I say, "It's the calcium deficiency. It makes his whole body ache."

"Oh, yes," the nurse registers. "I'll speak to the doctor." She turns on her soft heel and pads down the hall.

Later she comes to the room to confirm, "He can get it anytime he wants."

"How soon then?"

"Lunchtime."

The resident on call stops by to deliver the official figure—three milligrams. As needed. He seems surprised then offended when I press him further. He asks if I'm from the area.

When we're alone again, I see there's blood dripping from my father's left nostril, and I take a tissue from the box on the bed table. He still tries to raise himself, even to get out—at one point he manages to pull his legs over the side.

When I lift his head to settle him back on the pillow, the static silver strands cling to my fingers like Christmas angel hair. I used to wind the stuff around and around our family's tree until it looked like some fright from Miss Havisham's parlor, and Mother begged me to stop.

He's saying something, trying. I put my ear to his lips but still can't understand. It makes him impatient, his head tosses on the pillow and he strains upward, purses his lips to form the sounds with exaggerated slowness.

"D-A-D," he pronounces emphatically. His listener's so stupid he has to spell things.

"Oh. You're thinking of your father."

Yes. He lets go the tremendous effort of arching his body. Someone's understood. It's Dad.

I moisten his mouth with the lemon swab. He says "water"— maybe even "glass of water." But he turns his head when I try the straw between his lips.

He mutters into the pillow. It sounds like *car, car*, then a hissing: *gas*. The car's fine. Plenty of gas.

I tell him I found a place to park right on the street. Didn't even have to use the hospital garage this morning.

But he's gone. I'm left foolishly in conversation with myself.

He may have said his last words.

Neck arched on the pillow, mouth open so he exhales on a protracted moan. *Aaah.* I've heard it before through the wall at home when I use the middle room for my visits and he sleeps next door in my old bed. *Aaah, oh oh.* A running battle against his nightmare—or was he dying in there? I'd try the pillow over my head, dig in my nails.

By the time Mother's come and gone on her lunch hour he's simmered down, the fresh dose of morphine taking him under.

The oxygen bubbles in the tank beside his bed. Outside the heavy door there's the clatter of dish carts, news over the intercom, an orderly makes a date. I can read my book then and write something in my journal.

It's the middle of the afternoon when he comes to suddenly. His words distinct in the drowsy room.

"I keep forgetting who you are."

I touch the blanket.

"Don't worry. I'll remind you. I'm Wendy."

He sighs and lets his head sink back.

"Wendy, Wendy. It's always Wendy."

Mrs. Tate comes at four to take vital signs. She says he's probably already in a coma. They've upped the dosage to six. His numbers are still steady, but there's no response to touch.

We talk over him and around him, as if he weren't there. My mother was right—it *is* like a return to childhood.

Even when we're alone, I try to shush his sounds. Stroking him, his arm, his side, patting him down till he's quiet and good.

He is now. He's not moaning anymore exactly. It's just the ragged course of the fluids running in his throat.

The death rattle?

Mike comes. He says I didn't do the wrong thing. The higher dosage probably does facilitate coma but it's a kindness. He squeezes my shoulder.

Then an old student stops by just before five. He leaves a note: "I saw you were sleeping—*Güte Traumerein!*"

The airport where I drive the next day to pick up the featured speaker at her conference is outside the city limits, the conference center's the other way. A long ride. We don't mind though, Mother says, really, it's good to have a chance to relax, look at the nice scenery, talk about other things for a change.

Her guest says he's sorry about her husband.

This is a treat, though. He was expecting a secretary or someone like that to meet his flight. Now he'll have the extra time to bounce his new idea off Lillian.

It needs her special touch. He can talk concept, but she's the one who knows how to generate the language.

The Center's nestled in the woods. The gravel drive winds for more than a mile off the main highway, then the pines thin out where the line of slave cabins begins—he's never seen real slave quarters before has he?

These are some of the finest examples in the South. The original family donated them to the University along with the house and grounds. They're being restored for use by conference participants— it turns out people find them charming.

You've never even seen the old mansion from the inside, have you, Wendy, she says, they've done such interesting things with it, and you look lovely in that skirt you wore for the hospital, her conference people would enjoy meeting one of the daughters.

At least don't go right back there, then. He won't even know. Go home. Fix yourself a drink. Find a good book. There're new paperbacks on that shelf in the middle room, she puts them there each time she finishes one.

After six hospital parking's free. Only a few other cars, random in the echoing concrete tiers—whoever wouldn't leave or couldn't not come back.

I take an old transistor radio I brought and my notebook from the front seat and stuff them in my bag. My hand brushes the cardboard sign my mother brought back from the Diocesan Convention to hang from the rearview mirror:

Drive Carefully
You might hit an Episcopalian

He wouldn't like something dangling there like that, distracting the driver.

The attendant's cubicle is empty. I walk in the sound of my own steps, the bag bumping my side.

Clare thought of the radio. If she couldn't be with him at the end, she at least wanted to contribute something. His music. He might not hear it but he'd like the idea.

236

He's in the same position as before, a quiet curl against the bars. I set up in the chair. Book, notebook, radio on the bedside table, facing the speaker so the sound will go his way.

I switch it on and adjust the band. Mozart? Haydn? He'd have known. Late Haydn, early Mozart. Possibly some lesser contemporary of them both. He knew the stylistic conventions of each period, who exemplified them, who pushed at the limits or went beyond them. A few bars sometimes, a phrase, and he had it pinned down, composer, composition, even to the date, listening to the car radio as we waited—ten minutes, fifteen minutes, eighteen, how long could it take her?—in the driveway outside Mother's office window.

There was a quartet, a trio, something he wanted played at his funeral. What was it? Schubert? Schumann? He's told us so many times no one remembers.

His mouth's an O, a small dark hole with the buzz saw of a cartoon trailing out. He doesn't move when I touch the lemon Q-tip to his dry lips. He rests.

A vacuum cleaner tube knocks at the outside wall, then moves down the hall.

"When I say a *stiff* . . ." a male voice booms. Then female laughter.

Some helper in a smock pushes open the door. Stops there. A finger across her lips at what she sees. She nods, complicit with his visitor: Do Not Disturb.

I write it all down. Between times I talk to him. Mike said you never know.

"That boy was here—from your seminar, remember? The one with the funny ears."

"Dr. Grisholm from Church. You told him you could swear he'd gotten taller every Sunday, and then you were so embarrassed when he said he had that disease."

"You remember."

I sound like my mother. Like Clare sometimes, trying to joke him out of a mood. Sometimes like no one in our family, I call him *dear*, or *sweetheart*, daring words my lips form strangely.

Father Tom comes in at the beginning of the Brahms—the Third Symphony I learned in college for my Music History final. I listened to it over and over till I had it cold. The three-note figure rising in the strings, reaching for the the fifth, then the seventh, backing down, describing desire, longing for it.

The priest stands over my father on the opposite side of the bed, prayer book in one hand, the other resting on the sleeping shape. The window frames him. The sky's drained, there's a quiet interval out in the corridor as the day shift leaves and night comes on. He recites the Nunc Dimittis.

"We know that whether we live or die, we are in the palm of Your hand."

He asks God's blessings on Victor, on Victor's wife and children, and with his finger makes the sign of the Cross on the air and on the forehead of the sick man.

He was only driving by the hospital, he tells my mother later, but something made him stop in.

He touches the head.

"Depart, O Christian soul, out of this world, in the Name of God the Father Almighty who created you, God the Son who redeemed you, and God the Holy Spirit who sanctified you, forever and ever, Amen."

When we're alone again, I copy it down—the common prayer recovering the path of his life. Delivering him from it. The poetry of the faith he raised us in. I'm writing when he dies.

Fresh blood leaking from his nose when I look up.

I take a tissue to it but my hand stops.

Could he be so still?

How faint is breath?

He hugs himself so tight I can't fit my hand flat on his chest. I try my fingers against his neck, but it might not be the right place.

There's no one out in the hall. When I reach the nurses' station, I wait for their attention before the words come.

"I think someone should check on my father."

Mrs. Tate starts up from the duty desk. She orders the other one to

page the doctor on call then leads the way, her pliant soles as soft on the linoleum as the padded footfalls of the hound in Daddy's long-ago poem, who caught the scent of Christ in the honeysuckle hedge in Marshall.

The resident's there to meet us—so quick. They brush past me to take their places, one on either side, at the head of the bed. Mrs. Tate waits for the doctor's lead.

First he places two fingers at the throat, then they strip the sheet down and he finds the tender part at the back of an ankle. He lifts the slack lids to peer in anyway. A pinprick of light in each eye. Then the cold stethoscope underneath the breastbone, verifying the absolute remission of life at each station. He hangs up the instrument around his neck and, finally, puts his head down on the chest and listens the way I like to listen to certain records, my ear against the speaker to catch the last straining notes.

He raises up and checks his watch and the nurse, copying, consults her own bony wrist.

She says, "Do you want to call your mother?"

"Is he dead?"

The doctor nods his permission, and Mrs. Tate says, "Yes."

There's a cubby inside the nurses' station with a desk bare of everything but a box of tissues and the black phone. Mrs. Tate sits me down there and bows out the door, respectful.

University Information finds the number and puts me through to the conference center. They have to pass the message. It's a loud room. Later Mother says she's afraid she made a public spectacle.

A clatter, a fumble with the instrument, then her voice: "Hello? Hello?"

They've forgotten to tell her who's calling.

"It's Wendy, Mother."

It takes a moment for her to adjust.

"Wendy. Yes. How are you? Are you at home?" Laughter from the happy background. "Is everything all right?"

"I'm at the hospital, Mother. Mother, Daddy died tonight."

A crash when she drops the receiver. Other voices, people moving in, people moving furniture. Her wail is long and far away.

Did they break her fall? Did she hit her head on something, going down? Have I killed my mother?

There's a way to do things, a right way and a wrong way. You have to think before you open your mouth. You have to use your head.

Then she's back. They've helped her to the phone. People standing by.

"Oh Wendy. No. When? Oh, you were with him."

She sobs.

"I never had to watch a parent die."

She asks, "Should I come to the hospital?"

No, not at the hospital. Mrs. Tate's whisper in the corridor—"We can only keep the body in the room for an hour."

We'll meet at home.

There's a younger, blonde woman helping Mrs. Tate. A plain smock, no nameplate. I've seen her there before. A Jade or a Joy. Some kind of trainee.

They're trying to straighten him out. Opening his arms and pressing down on the legs. They reach all the way under the torso and shift the body more toward the center of the bed. The head lolls, his arms flop at his sides. They can't hurt him, but it makes him look more vulnerable.

They adjust his head on the pillow. Some last touches over the eyes. Then they stand back: someone's move.

Mrs. Tate says, "Do you want a moment alone with him?"

I study the women's handiwork.

He's fixed neatly, the sheet folded at the top and pulled tight under the armpits. His long arms are marred with bruises from so many needles. Shower-pale under the swirls of dark hair. The left wrist shaved for the implantation of the shunt. The silver ID chain he wore from his army days hangs from the other wrist. I slip it off over the sensitive right hand whose meanings I've learned so well.

240

The hand that guided me. That put the pen in my hand.

I stroke the fine silver head, then cautiously, with the back of my hand, his thin fallen-in cheek, the white seedlings of the beard Mother didn't want him to grow. He'll be more like his brother now. The phone on the bedside table rings. I have to go around to answer.

It's from inside the hospital somewhere, another department. They want to know about the eyes.

But he never said, he never wrote it down, he wouldn't like it—Mother wouldn't. He'd want his eyes buried with the rest of him. I tell the man no.

My time must be running out.

But I sit in my old chair, staying with the body.

Then I reach across the bed to touch him once more. I tell him good-bye for my mother, good-bye for Margaret, good-bye for Clare. I kiss the cool forehead.

The suit, the tie, the leather slippers, loose change for the paperboy, glasses, pens, paper tablets, books from the radiator sill. One pair of clean blue pajamas—Mrs. Tate slides his wedding ring through the watchband and tucks them both in the pocket. There's the medicine cabinet too, everything from his razor to the styptic pencil. He must have hoped for at least one more upright morning at the mirror.

We load the suitcase onto the cart parked out in the hallway, piling the books underneath and wedging the bottle of sherry between them. The blonde nurse hands me a pillowcase stuffed with soiled underwear and T-shirts bloody from where he tried to get at his itching back. I stick it in with the books.

I trundle his things down the hall. Squeaky wheels. Spongy footsteps following me. I'm stopped at the elevator, caught by the sleeve—it's Joy.

She's upset. We *must* talk.

She got to know my father before he died, he seemed to feel close to her. He even thought she and I might become friends.

She says he knew I would be there at the end. He wanted Joy to give me a message: seek religion.

We hike the cart over the ledge of the elevator and take it down to the ground floor together. Joy offers to wait while I go to get his car.

A soft rain drops on the Victorless night.

It doesn't take long—one of us handing things off to the other.

I slide in behind the wheel and turn the key. Then the wipers to clear the blurred windshield. I look back to wave my thanks.

The strange woman's crying.

A migh-ty for-tress is our God,
A bul-wark nev-er fail-ing . . .

We shared hymnals, holding them up on either side—Clare and Margaret, Lillian and Wendy. *Your four women, Daddy.*

Earlier that morning when I went out to get the newspaper at the end of the driveway for Mother's breakfast tray, I heard the unreal birds singing in January. The trees were dripping. The sky cleared by the time we drove the block to St. Ann's. People stopped us in the parking lot on our way in, smiling and crying, shaking our hands as if to congratulate us.

Did we in our own strength confide
Our stri-ving would be los-ing . . .

The coffin was a modest pine box. Margaret and I had chosen it when we met with the undertaker at the funeral home—Clare and Mother would have gotten too upset. Later when they went with us to see him there for the last time, Mother tucked his Robert E. Lee medallion into his shirt pocket. Now the casket sat in front of the congregation on the first step of the altar throughout the long service so that we prayed and sang to it.

Let goods and kindred go,
This mortal life also;
The body they may kill:
God's truth abideth still,
His kingdom is for-ev-er.

Everything he'd been—all he'd given us, taken from us, de-manded—it all fit inside a box.
My hand holding the hymnal started to shake.
My mother reached over. I felt her fingers on my wrist.
Her soft skin, that touch I needed a long, long time ago.
"Are you all right?"
I stopped singing. I was dizzy—taking in too much air, trying to be heard above the others in that childish boy soprano I'd never quite lost, that used to thrill my mother so.

Acknowledgments

I thank the MacDowell Colony for the gift of time and space. Thanks to Roya Hakakian for having faith in my work and for introducing me to my agent, Glen Hartley; to Glen for his dedication and hard work, and to my editor, Gillian Blake, for her amazing radar.

I'm grateful to Robin Schindler, for listening; to the wonderful friends who have read this book and encouraged me over the years, and whose work and lives inspire me every day: Cynthia Keyworth, Jennifer Jarrett, Lew Hyde, Nan Morrison, Mila Drumke, Brenda Currin, Karl Kirchwey, Miranda Beverly-Whittemore, and especially Jane Mankiewicz, without whose friendship and generosity this book would never have been written.

Finally, I thank my nieces, Mary and Caitlin, and my nephew Liam, who've brought me so much happiness, and who carry the best of everything into the future.

A Note on the Author

Wendy Salinger is the author of *Folly River*, which won the National Poetry Series, and a graduate of Duke University and the University of Iowa. Her work has appeared in the *New Yorker*, the *Kenyon Review*, the *Paris Review*, and *Ploughshares*. She is the recipient of a Guggenheim Fellowship and has been a fellow at the MacDowell Colony. She directs the Schools Project at the 92nd St. Y's Unterberg Poetry Center in New York City.

A Note on the Type

Linotype Garamond Three is based on seventeenth-century copies of Claude Garamond's types, cut by Jean Jannon. This version was designed for American Type Founders in 1917 by Morris Fuller Benton and Thomas Maitland Cleland, and adapted for mechanical composition by Linotype in 1936.